# Farewell
## to the
# Founder

R. G. Moyles

CREST BOOKS

*Salvation Army National Publications*
*615 Slaters Lane*
*Alexandria, Virginia 22313*

Published by Crest Books
The Salvation Army National Headquarters
615 Slaters Lane
Alexandria, VA 22313
Phone: 703/684-5523
Fax: 703/302-8617

Major Allen Satterlee, Editor in Chief and National Literary Secretary
Judith L. Brown, Crest Books Coordinator
Lisa Jones, Cover Design
Available from The Salvation Army Supplies and Purchasing Departments
    Des Plaines, IL – (847) 937-8896
    West Nyack, NY – (888) 488-4882
    Atlanta, GA – (800) 786-7372
    Long Beach, CA – (847) 937-8896

Printed in the United States of America

ISBN: 978-0-9831482-4-1
Library of Congress Control Number: 2011943656

Cover reproduced from the *War Cry*, September 14, 1912, USA

# Contents

# Introduction

Nothing is here for tears, nothing to wail
Or knock the breast, no weakness, no contempt,
Dispraise, or blame; nothing but well and fair,
And what may quiet us in a death so noble.

John Milton, *Samson Agonistes*

When William Booth, Founder and General of the Salvation Army, died at 10:13 p.m. on August 20, 1912, the world went immediately into mourning, lamenting the loss of one of the greatest evangelists and perhaps the most brilliant social reformer of the nineteenth century.

Newspapers in every civilized nation made the announcement of his death front-page headlines; every editorial eulogized his achievements; a few even devoted whole issues to retrospective assessments of his career. Messages of condolence poured in to International Headquarters from the far corners of the earth, from presidents and prime ministers, emperors and kings, church leaders and politicians.

As his body lay resting for a four-day public viewing at the Clapton Congress Hall, surrounded by an honor-guard of

Salvationists, more than 100,000 people, representing all classes of society, queued for many hours to pay their respects. At the memorial service held in the London Olympia on August 28, some 25,000 Salvationists, wearing white arm-bands, renewed their promises of allegiance, as they *celebrated* their General's life and remembered his personal impact on their own lives. And on the day of his funeral, August 29, an estimated *two million* people lined the streets of the city of London on an afternoon officially designated a public half-holiday, as the mile-long funeral procession made its five-mile trip to Abney Park cemetery. It was, most observers agreed, as impressive a funeral as any ever witnessed in that city.

What follows is a full and comprehensive account of William Booth's death and funeral, describing his final moments on earth, the world's immediate reaction, the range and depth of the tributes, the poignancy of the public viewing, the celebratory spirit of the memorial service, the impressiveness of the funeral and, finally, the subsequent speculation about the future of The Salvation Army without its beloved leader. The inclination to pursue this subject does not arise out of any sense of morbid curiosity, nor should any reader think that such a state of mind is necessary to read about it.

The interest arises mainly from a desire to understand the amazing respect and love which General Booth elicited not only from Salvationists but from the public at large; to see just how the Army, through his leadership and personality, had risen from a much maligned, even detested, organization to one which had secured the admiration of most world leaders; and finally to get a sense of what, in the opinions of many commentators, the impact of the General's death would have on the future of the Army. For his death was, in many ways, both an end and a beginning.

It must be admitted, of course, that much of what was written on that occasion took the form of eulogy or encomia—unabashed praise—and writers may have, out of respect for the dead, ignored for the moment any negative opinions they may have harbored. They may, in other words, have been less objective than they might have been on any other occasion. In spite of that caution, however, the subject of Booth's death and funeral, buttressed though it is with subjective commentary, is still worth examining.

For its own sake, first of all, to see just how universal were the tributes and how sincerely loved the man was; and, more important, to see through all the reverence and hyperbole, the eminence this lowly man had achieved and the reasons why he had done so. As George Eliot put it, "Oh may I join the choir invisible/Of those immortal dead who live again/In minds made better by their presence." In other words, by remembering William Booth's death we can catch a glimpse of his purpose and passion and be ennobled by it.

*In William Booth's last public address, he said: "The Army will not be allowed to suffer, either financially or spiritually, or in any other way in my absence."*

## CHAPTER ONE

# "I'll Fight to the Very End"

All those who knew William Booth well agreed that his was a boundless and restless energy. Simply put, he could not, would not, allow a moment to pass without trying, in some way or other, to "save souls." From the day on which he established his Christian Mission on July 5, 1865, through to the inspirational moment when he changed its name to the Salvation Army in 1878, he had toiled unceasingly to "win the world for God." He had molded his converts into a fighting unit, had put them in uniforms and set them marching through the streets; he had planted his flag in every major country in the world and had visited most; and, on top of it all, he had instituted a system of social reform which had rescued millions from poverty and sin.

## NARY A HOLIDAY

He had never taken a holiday and had only stopped working on the very few occasions when sickness forced him to rest. He had no time, he often said, to think of death—he was too busy to do so. And though he was, in 1912, in his eighty-fourth year, and though his physical powers had somewhat waned and his sight almost left him, his determination to keep "fighting"—to lead his soldiers by example, to keep travelling as their spiritual overseer, to still preach and write—was as strong as ever. As one of his officers put it, just two weeks before his death, "his marvelous energy astonishes us all."

To the casual observer, it might have seemed, as early as 1909, that William Booth's active career as evangelist and spiritual leader was practically over. For early in that year he began to lose his sight. After a cataract operation in February, which afforded him a brief respite, in August an infection of the right eye (probably from an insect bite while he was on his sixth motor-car crusade) necessitated its removal and soon afterward his left eye began to fail. The nearly two years remaining to him were to be spent in virtual darkness.

But, again, true to character, such a serious debility in no way slowed him down or dampened his enthusiasm for the mission. Even his moments of mild despair he managed to pass off with characteristic humor. "I feel," he wrote in his diary, "as though I were some old vessel that had run on to some rock and was being dashed to pieces by the storming waves, while the crew were considering the propriety of her abandonment, and the proprietors were arguing in their own minds as to the value of the salvage."

Or, more often, he met them with renewed resolve. "Never again to see the light of day!" he wrote, "Never again to witness that which, for sixty years gone by, has been to me the sight of sights—men and women kneeling at the Mercy Seat! Well, the Lord's will be done. I have done my best for my God and for the

*William Booth met with Home Secretary Winston Churchill in 1910, about plans to establish a prison ministry.*

people with my eyes; now, if it is His will, I must do my best for Him without my eyes." [See Wiggins, Vol. 5, p. 237].

## FAILING SIGHT

This William Booth most certainly did. While he still had partial sight (though it was quickly fading), and though depending more urgently on his younger assistants, he adhered to a taxing schedule. Early in 1910 he preached in Holland, Germany and Scandinavia, attracting huge crowds. On his eightieth birthday in April of that year, he talked of having written several "birthday reflections" for various Army publications: "I endeavored to put into every message I sent some real Salvation Army doctrine, and to urge each person's responsibility for their own salvation and the salvation of their neighbors." Not long after, he was again in Europe, on another "continental campaign" and then, for the remainder of the year, he worked to establish a prison ministry with visits to Scotland and a meeting with the Home Secretary, Winston Churchill. It was not, perhaps, as active a year as many previous, but, for a nearly-blind eighty-one year old, it was quite an industrious and productive one.

Nor was 1911 any less so. That year was highlighted by yet another cross-country "motor campaign" (his seventh), commencing where the 1909 campaign had abruptly ended because of his eye trouble. Starting out at Leigh, Lancashire, on August 27, and ending at Cardiff, three weeks later, he managed yet another successful 1600-mile promotional and preaching tour of England. On either side of that astonishing feat, he conducted a two-week evangelistic campaign in Europe (including Italy), presided over the Army's first International Social Council (attended by delegates from around the world), undertook a series of seaside campaigns at Southport—all this in addition to his many preaching stints (of up to an hour and a quarter in length), and dozens of personal interviews.

## "WHERE ARE WE, SMITH?"

He was resilient. In the final months of his life, General Booth was not only nearly blind, but also suffered from occasional blackouts. His private secretary, Major Evan Smith, tells how the General even then refused to admit defeat:

> One seizure came on prior to the Sunday evening meeting, during a campaign that was being held in the largest theater in Newcastle. We were having tea in the home of Sir George Hunter, where we were being entertained for the weekend, when I led the General upstairs to his bedroom to have some rest.

The meeting was announced to commence at 6:30 p.m., but when that time arrived there was no sign of recovery, and there were 5,000 or more people crammed into that large building awaiting the General's arrival. I phoned Commissioner John Lawley to say that the General was too ill to come immediately, and suggested that he should go on with the preliminaries and I would bring the General as soon as possible.

Ultimately the General recovered sufficiently for us to proceed to the carriage in which Sir George was waiting for us, and as we were driving along, by question and answer, the General's memory gradually returned. "Where are we, Smith?" "You are going to preach tonight." "What on?" "Jonah, General." "Jonah! Ah, yes, Jonah."

Although arriving at the theater an hour late, the General was given a rousing welcome as he stepped upon the stage, and after the

*"It was hard to believe that the white-haired prophet who paced up and down the platform could not see a face in the front row."*

*crowd had ended a verse of the song they had been singing, he rose
to his feet and delivered a sermon, unsurpassed for vividness and
power by any previous effort I had ever heard.*

## EIGHTY-THIRD BIRTHDAY

General Booth's perseverance continued unabated to the very
end. Early in 1912 he conducted a series of public and staff meetings in Holland and later in Oslo (then Christiana), Norway,
where he also lectured at the university. On April 10, the occasion
of his eighty-third birthday, he wrote in his journal: "Eighty-third
birthday! It seems almost incredible, but there is the remarkable
fact, and poorly as I am, on and off, everybody considers it next
to a miracle that I should be so young and energetic and capable
of so much work, and ever so many other things."

By that time, however, his sight had almost completely failed,
with only a slight possibility that an operation scheduled for May
might minimally restore it. So, at his birthday celebration (and
salvation meeting) held in the Clapton Congress Hall, for which
his daughter, Eva, had travelled from the United States, he tacitly
admitted that this might be his last public function and perhaps
his last address to his people.

The several thousand people who had assembled heard him
say, "And now, comrades and friends, I must say goodbye. I am
going into dry-dock for repairs, but the Army will not be allowed
to suffer, either financially or spiritually, or in any other way by
my absence; and in the long future I think it will be seen—and I
will not be here to see—but you will, that the Army will answer
every doubt and banish every fear and strangle every slander, and
by its marvelous success show to the world that it is the work of
God and that The General has been his servant."

But, though forced to say a tentative "goodbye" he nevertheless renewed his promise, and revived his listeners' spirits, by

uttering what became his best-remembered, and most often quoted, commitment:

> *While women weep, as they do now, I'll fight; while little children go hungry, as they do now, I'll fight; while men go into prison, in and out, in and out, as they do now, I'll fight; while there is a drunkard left, while there is a poor lost girl upon the streets, while there remains one dark soul without the light of God, I'll fight—I'll fight to the very end.*

As one reporter observed, "It was hard to believe that the white-haired prophet who paced up and down the platform as he poured forth his warnings and appeals could not see a face in the front row. The voice, however husky, was the authentic voice of an apostle." [Wilson, *General Evangeline Booth*, p. 57].

## EYE SURGERY

William Booth's "birthday" address did indeed prove to be his last. On May 23, 1912, he once again submitted to an operation which, it was hoped, would restore at least partial sight. Unfortunately, the procedure failed. When his son, Bramwell, broke the news to him he bore it with a moment of silence before rallying his courage to assert: "Well, Bramwell, I've done what I could for God and for the people *with* my eyes—now I shall do what I can for God and for the people *without* my eyes." "Such was the indomitable courage of this great soldier of Jesus Christ," wrote his private secretary. "Nothing could divert him from pursuing his God-given task" [Smith, p. 126].

As, indeed, it could not. For, amazingly, as soon he had recovered his strength (thanks to the tender care of his youngest daughter, Lucy), his zeal again began to reassert itself. "I am hoping," he told a delegation of his senior officers, "to be able to talk to my officers and help them all over the world. I am still hoping to go to America and Canada, as I bargained for. I am hoping for several things, whether they come to pass or not" [Begbie, 424]. And in a letter to his daughter, Eva, he was equally optimistic:

> *So, I am going to make another attempt at work. What do you think of that? I have sat down this afternoon, not exactly to the desk, but anyway to the duties of the desk, and I am going to strive to stick to them if I possibly can. I have been down to some of my meals; I have had a walk in the garden, and now it is proposed for me to take a drive in a motor, I believe some kind soul is loaning me. Anyhow, I am going to have some machine that will shuffle me along the street, road, and square, and I will see how that acts on my nerves, and then perhaps try something more [Begbie, p. 426].*

There were, of course, moments of anguish, much pain, and even despair, but most conspicuous, shining through it all, was his resolute determination to play his part to the end. Sometimes it manifested itself in his old quick reactions, as when one morning, during a serious strike in east London, his caregiver brought him an egg for breakfast. Pushing it away, he declared, "How can I eat eggs when women and children are starving! Poor women can't get milk to feed their babies, and you bring me an egg!" That was vintage William Booth. As was one of his last conversations with his son, Bramwell.

"One afternoon," writes Harold Begbie, "Bramwell Booth found his father sitting up in his arm-chair, evidently waiting to speak to him. What followed is the more touching for the fact that it proved to be William Booth's last consecutive conversation. The old warrior, greeting his son very quietly, said to him, "Chief, can you spare me a few moments? There are two matters much upon my mind. I want you to make me a promise concerning them." Then, as Bramwell Booth sat down near his father's chair, the General said, "Now, are you attending me?" and the conversation proceeded as follows:

# THE PROMISE

"I want you to promise me that when my voice is silent and I am gone from you, you will use such influence as you may possess with the Army to do more for the homeless of the world. The homeless men. Mind! I am not thinking of this country only, but of all the lands."

"Yes, General, I understand."

"The homeless women" and, with deepening tones, "Ah, my boy, we don't know what it means to be without a home."

"Yes, General, I follow."

"The homeless children. Oh, the children! Bramwell, *look after the* homeless. Promise me."

When the promise had been given, something of the old whimsical humor appeared as he exclaimed, "Mind! If you don't, I shall come back and haunt you!"

The extraordinary will to live and be useful meant that the end, when it came at thirteen minutes past ten o'clock on the evening of August 20, 1912, was a swift and peaceful one. George Scott Railton described it this way:

> *It was, perhaps, the greatest triumph of his own unfailing faith and sunny optimism that he kept even those who were nearest to him full of hope as to his complete recovery of strength till within a few days of his death; and then, gliding down into the valley, surprised all by sinking suddenly into eternal peace without any distinct warning that the end was so near.*

# VIOLENT STORM

"He lay very still and quiet," writes Harold Begbie, his best biographer, "as the last days of earthly life passed over him. He made no sign of a desire to speak. During the afternoon of August 20, a violent thunderstorm broke over the house, much like the storm that had marked the end of Catherine Booth's life. He made no sign. The storm passed, the quiet succeeded. In the evening there was a marked quickening of the breath and a weakening of the pulse. Bramwell turned to the doctor and asked if this were death.

"'Yes,' replied the doctor, 'this is death.' There was a movement among the watchers. Bramwell bent over his father and kissed him. 'Kiss him again,' whispered Mrs. Booth-Hellberg, 'kiss him for Eva.' And Bramwell kissed his father again, and placed in his hand the cable which had come from Eva in America, saying: 'Kiss him for me.' That was the end of the vigil."

Though it was a peaceful passing, one whose eternal reward had been assured, there were many moments of tender affection and understandable sadness as family and friends kept vigil in those final days. One of those who did was Colonel Fred Cox who, for seven years (1901-1908), had been Booth's private secretary, accompanying him on his many journeys around the world, not only getting to know him intimately, but loving him without reservation. Cox was called from Wales on August 19.

No one will ever know what feelings surged up within him as he entered that room where William Booth lay unconscious beneath the flag which he had unfurled on Calvary. Cox saluted, then bending over the bed he kissed his beloved leader on brow and hand. There followed a long conversation with Bramwell Booth, who told him how in these last days the old man had called repeatedly: "Cox! Cox! I want you!"—just as Cox himself had heard it so often in days gone by.

That night [August 20] Cox was one of the privileged few in the old General's room. He says:

*There as I stood spellbound, with clasped hands at the foot of the bed, me thought I saw the Unseen Angel saluting as my General passed into the Great Beyond. Then there flashed into my minds the lines:*

DEATH SALUTED!
"Pass in," he softly cried,
The General heard
The General stirred,
Man said, "The General died,"
Man erred and DEATH SALUTED!

*Bramwell Booth had said to me on one occasion: "You know, Cox, I want yours to be the hand to close the dear old man's eyes in death," but though it was not mine to do so—for blindness had intervened— yet mine were the feet that stood that night in the death chamber, and mine the ears that heard his last sigh, and mine the lips that kissed his icy brow, and mine the finger that arranged his snow-white hair, and mine the eyes that saw him pass into the Saints' Reward. And mine the hands that laid out the old man's earthly tabernacle, and arrayed it in his uniform, and left him lying . . . "like a warrior taking his rest, with his martial cloak around him."*

## THE BOOTH CHILDREN

The only children to keep vigil at his deathbed were his daughter, Lucy Booth-Hellberg and his son, Bramwell. Lucy had nursed him through his final days, and had sung to him as often as he requested. Bramwell had been his prayer support. Both were towers of strength. Eva, unfortunately, having to travel by ocean liner from New York, could not see the father she adored before he passed and would only arrive just before the funeral service.

The only sad note of the moment, kindly ignored by most observers, was the absence of his other children, Herbert, Catherine and Ballington. Herbert, living in America, was also late arriving, but even if he had arrived earlier, he might not have been allowed into the death chamber. For, having been estranged for some eight years now, he might have been treated like his sister, Catherine. When she, also a "deserter" from the Army's ranks (a

*Catherine had to keep her identity a*
*secret from her dying father.*

harsh term not wholly deserved), arrived at Hadley Wood, asking
to see her father, she was at first refused.

"It was thought [most likely by Bramwell] that the shock
would be too much for him. 'I must go to him,' she insisted, and
eventually she was allowed into his room on condition that she
would not say who she was. The General was lying in bed, his
hair white, his fingers moving constantly: the gesture she remembered so well as he had counted the numbers coming forward to
the old Whitechapel penitent benches. As she bent over him, he
stirred and asked, 'Who is it?' but she looked at him for a long
time and then, keeping her promise, came away without answer-
ing." [*The Heavenly Witch*, p. 217]. The third son, Ballington, who
had left the Army in 1896 and lived in New York as head of The
Volunteers of America, sent only a brief message of condolence.

*At the time of his father's death, Herbert Booth had already resigned from the Salvation Army. He lived in America and had been estranged from his father for eight years.*

Of these small family matters the public had no knowledge. It was enough to know, as the notice outside International Headquarters proclaimed, that General William Booth had "laid down his sword." They would soon be assured, as Salvationists already were, that Death had no sting. The next few days would therefore be given over not to mourning but to celebration, the celebration of a life fully lived in the service of God.

"*General Booth made his last march with 6,000 soldiers before him. It was a march of triumph.*"

## CHAPTER TWO

# "The General is Dead, Long Live the General"

When William Booth was asked, as he so often was, "What will happen when you die, General? Who will take on your work?" he always replied, "The same electric flash that tells the world the General is dead will announce the name of his successor." The two events, in actuality, were not that simultaneous but nearly so. For, as in the case of monarchies—to which the Salvation Army bore a striking resemblance—obsequies for the dead were, for the moment, held in abeyance until the matter of the succession could be settled.

Since it was not known (as it would have been with a king or queen) who the successor was, it was necessary to invoke a legal procedure known as "opening the white envelope." By the terms of the 1878 Deed Poll, the choice of successor was the sole prerogative of the Founder, and on August 21, 1890, William Booth, after consulting with his dying wife, had placed the name of his successor in an envelope and had sealed it in the presence of and delivered it for safekeeping to the Army's solicitor, Dr. Washington Ranger.

It was necessary, therefore, to engage in a brief legal ceremony, which took place at four o'clock on the afternoon of August 21, 1912. At that time Bramwell Booth, as Chief of Staff, arranged to meet with Dr. Ranger and his partner, Mr. Frost, for the purpose of opening the so-called "white envelope." Present were Bramwell's wife, Florence, and ten Commissioners then in London: Lucy Booth-Hellberg, T. Henry Howard, John A. Carleton, George S. Railton, Edward J. Higgins, Elijah Cadman, Adelaide Cox, Thomas McKie, Hugh Whatmore and Randolph Burgess.

## OPENING THE ENVELOPE

After prayer, Dr. Ranger produced the envelope, which he said had been handed to him just twenty-two years ago on that very day. After he had passed it around so that the signature on the outside might be verified, he opened the envelope without breaking the seal by slitting it open at the opposite end. Mr. Frost then read the document which, as many expected, formally declared Bramwell Booth to be the General's successor. When Dr. Ranger asked him if he accepted the appointment, Bramwell Booth "replied as best he could with deep emotion, accepting the appointment and expressing his keen sense of the great loss the Army had sustained and his resolution, by God's grace, to carry out faithfully the new responsibilities thus cast upon him" [*Times*, Aug. 22].

After each Commissioner had spoken words of support, Dr. Ranger announced that all legal formalities had been observed and that Bramwell Booth was henceforth, in fact and in law, the new General of the Salvation Army.

## BRAMWELL'S ACCEPTANCE

The brief ceremony concluded with Bramwell's short address to those assembled:

*My comrades, I accept this appointment; I do so even if no other consideration moved me to that course because it was my "General's" wish, and I am strengthened in that purpose because of the fact of which I had no knowledge until a few moments ago, that this appointment was made during the lifetime of my beloved mother. I can only hope in the strength and wisdom of God to enable me to discharge the responsibilities which I am now taking upon myself. I cast myself upon Him and invoke His aid. And next to His help I must rely upon yours and the help of those whom you represent, and as earnestly as I can I cast myself upon you and invoke your aid.*

*I think I ought to say here that I promise, in the strength of God, that I will, to the full measure of my ability, discharge the obligations which this office imposes upon me. I accept it, and I declare that it is my best intention to discharge those obligations as they are set forth in our foundation documents. I will do this in the fear of God and out of love for the Army, and out of regard to the memory of him whose thoughts and purposes those instruments express.*

*You will not expect me to speak of him today. I confess that my heart is too much moved with present grief at our great loss—a loss we can only too faintly estimate as we stand here; but I felt last night as we closed his eyes, and I saw him pass away, that here was a concluded life of splendid conflict for righteousness, and, may I not add, a life of splendid triumph for the cause of Christ? It would be difficult to look out on the world in any direction, with such hearts as we have, and not feel that it is a poor place for us, but it would have been vastly poorer if he had never lived and blessed it.*

*I must, with the whole strength of my heart, ask you to help me and my dear wife, who is with me in all that I say, and so far as God shall enable us, will accept these obligations with a single eye for His glory, for the blessing of the world, and for the salvation of the people. Dr. Ranger, my dear comrades, I accept the appointment of "General." [Times, Aug. 22].*

## INDISPENSABLE KITCHENER

Commenting on the succession, the London *Times* had this to say: "No living person has been so closely and intimately concerned with the actual administration of the Army as the Chief of Staff. Nobody, perhaps, since the death of Mrs. Booth, has shared the confidence of the late 'General' and aided and interpreted his policy more than his eldest son. Probably there was no single member of the Army, from the experienced staff officers in Queen Victoria Street down to the humblest drummer in a village band, who imagined that any other chief than Mr. Bramwell Booth was possible.

"Mr. Bramwell Booth has been for many years the business head of the Salvation Army. He has been described as 'the indispensable Kitchener' of the organization, and the author of this phrase has further written, 'I have no hesitation in declaring that without his executive nous [mind] and skill and his contentment to occupy the most onerous and thankless of offices, it would have been humanly impossible for 'General' Booth to have given cohesion and uniformity to the many departments that had to be created.'

"Mr. Booth, while a devoted Salvationist and a man of spiritual power, is also an excellent businessman. He has been Chief of Staff for 32 years, and undoubtedly the Army owes much to his genius for organization, his cool, alert judgment, and his loyalty to the 'General,' his father . . . The father typified the genius and dash of the Salvation Army to the outside world; the son was, for the Army itself, the center of authority and the permanent executive power" (Aug. 22).

"He was alone with an idea that burned at a white heat and consumed all that lay in its path."

## CHAPTER THREE

# Tributes of Praise

For the first two days after his death, General Booth's body reposed in what the newspapers referred to as his "death chamber" which was, in reality, his bedroom at Rookstone, his Hadley Wood residence, where he lay dressed in full uniform. "The long white hair and full beard flowed around the marble-like face and over the black tunic, and the hands were crossed on his breast." At the foot of the bed stood two officers holding flags, while at the head of the bed was the flag General Booth had carried to Calvary on his visit in 1905.

"The room was almost exactly as when 'General' Booth rested there during his illness. The chair of green upholstery, on which he used to sit, remained; and above the mantlepiece there was a large photograph of his two daughters, Mrs. Booth-Hellberg (chief of the Army in Denmark) and Miss Eva Booth, who conducted the services in America. Resting on the mantlepiece was a portrait of Mrs. Booth, who died in 1890" [Times, Aug. 23].

## NOTABLES

Though there were many callers at the Hadley Wood home, only members of the family and privileged high-ranking officers (those who knew him personally or had worked directly under him) were allowed to "pay their respects" with a personal viewing. Others—among them messengers and equerries of high-ranking people—left their floral tributes and messages of condolence, among the first of them being from Britain's King George V:

> *I am grieved to hear the sad news of the death of your father. The nation has lost a great organizer and the poor a wholehearted and sincere friend, who devoted his life to helping them in a practical way. Only in the future shall we realize the good wrought by him for his fellow creatures. Today there is universal mourning for him. I join in it, and assure you and your family of my true sympathy in the heavy loss which has befallen you.*

And from Queen Alexandra (wife of King Edward VII and the mother of King George V), whose personal friendship William Booth had cherished:

> *I beg you and all your family to accept my deepest sympathy in the irreparable loss you and the nation have sustained in the death of your great, good, and never-to-be-forgotten father—a loss which will be felt throughout the whole civilized world. But, thank God! His work will live forever.*

Subsequently, when the news had reached across Britain and round the world, similar messages, with floral tributes, poured in from its farthest corners—from President Taft of the United States:

> *In the death of your good father the world loses one of its most effective and practical philanthropists. His long life and great talents*

*were dedicated to the noble work of helping the poor and weak and giving them another chance to attain success and happiness. Accept my deepest sympathy.*

Similar expressions of sympathy came from General Botha of South Africa, King Christian of Sweden, Prince Bernadotte of Stockholm, Lord Islington, the Governor of New Zealand, and from almost every notable world leader—governors and lieutenant-governors, prime ministers and premiers, state governors and

*Britain's King George V, who reigned from 1910–1936, sent a four foot floral wreath, which was placed at the head of the coffin.*

city mayors, archbishops and bishops, and literally thousands of common people.

In the days immediately following William Booth's death, the world's newspapers graphically informed their readers of the full details of his final moments.

They described, as best they could, the "bedside scenes," the family presence at the deathbed, and the tearful farewells. "Only a year ago," commented the London *Daily Express,* "he was rushing round the land in a motor-car, vigorously haranguing thousands of people about their souls. Now he is dead."

A few made mention of "The Sealed Envelope" which contained the name of his successor, and generally concluded that his eldest son, Bramwell, would be the new General. And still others looked for the touches of pathos which so often mark such an event, one of these concerning the fidelity of the General's dog, Gyp:

> *Tragedy and pathos are associated with little Gyp, the grief-stricken dog who had been the constant companion of General Booth. The General was deeply attached to Gyp, who for days past had been sitting at the gate of his master's house on Lancaster Avenue— sometimes for hours at a stretch—wearing a mournful expression, and throwing glances of mute and common sympathy to bark quietly, and give an appealing glance that seemed to inquire, "Where is my master?"*
>
> *Gyp fails to understand the long absence of the General, who was wont to play with him affectionately. He does not yet realize that he has seen the last of his master. The stroking of his shaggy, bristling hair and the attentions showered upon him do not raise his spirits [Daily Mirror, Aug. 22].*

## A GLOBAL OUTPOURING

Following such items, and generally in the midst of them, came the thoughtful tributes. On the front pages, and in the edi-

torials, of the London Times, the New York Herald, the Toronto
Star, across the nations of the world in the local dailies, praise for
the "fallen warrior" pushed all other news aside. They no wise
stinted their admiration for his remarkable career and contribu-
tion to society. The editor of the *Daily Graphic,* for example, had
this to say:

*The death of William Booth removes a very remarkable personality*
*from a world that certainly is the better for his life and work. This*

*Queen Alexandra, wife of Edward VII, was a per-*
*sonal friend of William Booth and a strong ally*
*of the Salvation Army.*

is a tribute that can rarely be paid in full measure to men and women, great in whatever sphere of human activity, as their turn comes to be called from the field of their labors.

That it belongs in highest degree to General Booth very few, we think, will be inclined to deny. He has had his critics. He has had his detractors. Their voice is drowned not only in the flood of gratitude that has arisen from the countless thousands of souls to whom his work has ministered, but in the approval and sympathy with which he has met from the highest quarters in every portion of the civilized globe.

When, indeed, the Salvation Army and its wonderful organization for rescuing the submerged is viewed as a whole, a feeling little short of amazement is aroused that it can be the original work of one man, carried out from inception to completion . . . To realize the magnitude of the task one has only to ask what possible chance of accomplishing a similar mission would await a young man without influence and without means who today started out with the intention that animated General Booth through youth, manhood, sickness, and old age, and that was fierce as ever within him as he lay on his death-bed. The answer would be that the task was insurmountable. He surmounted it.

## Secret of Success

Perhaps, in this connection, we may find the secret of his success in the fact that it was no final, definite end at which he aimed. He simply battled from year to year, day to day, hour to hour, with the forces of irreligion as he saw them. There was no goal of ultimate earthly victory before him, no point towards which he looked as the end of his labors and well deserved rest. He fought on—and the Salvation Army as we know it today arose around him as a natural process of his fighting. In any walk of life his talents must have placed him in the highest position. He dedicated them solely and unceasingly to the service of God.

"It was the triumph of General Booth," wrote the editor of the *Daily Express*, "to beat down by nobility of character and achievement a sea of prejudice which must have drowned a lesser man. He and the Salvation Army represented at one time, even to earnest Christians, a drum-beating and cymbal-clashing movement of hysterical and misapplied religiosity. Many years before he died he was able to know himself secure in the respect and affection of all who valued true religion and sound social work, to see the Salvation Army established firmly as a great religious and social organization, doing great service in all lands.

*William Howard Taft, President of the United States from 1909–1913, sent his condolences.*

"The man himself was one in whom the giant spirit found an ally in the invincible frame. The loss that his death means to the movement of which he was for so long the heart and soul, is incalculable. The loss to the world is very real, and really felt. Master of his fate and captain of his soul, he was a light to much darkness and an inexhaustible fount of energy." (Aug. 21).

The *Daily News* suggested that "Whatever may be the fate of the great fabric which he created, General William Booth will remain one of the most remarkable in the religious history of the modern world. His career has that quality of independence and isolation that is the hallmark of great creative minds.

"It owed nothing to others; it was indifferent to conventions and traditions and schools; it flashed across the sky on an orbit of its own that nothing could deflect. He began his amazing crusade amidst the brick-bats and ribaldry of the East-End, he ended it amidst the sanction of the whole world; but throughout he remained careless of the verdict of men . . . He was alone with an idea that burned at a white heat and consumed all that lay in its path" (Aug. 21).

The *Westminster Gazette* was similarly eulogistic. "Patriotism," it stated, "need not mean the warfare of banded legions, destructive combinations and all the details of preparedness for war in the name of peace. There is a higher patriotism. And this Man, now gone onward to his great rest was, perhaps, the highest exemplar of that highest patriotism. For he found in the festering dens of sin and crime the one eternal spark of Hope and fanned it into flame.

## GOLDEN DUSTMAN

"With winnowing hand he sifted chaff and grain, and deep in the soil of regeneration dedicated the seeds of self respect, self-sacrifice, and consecration to an Ideal which was not the less ideal that those who materialized it from want and misery could hardly spell the word. Like the 'golden dustman' of Dickens, he found and rescued the 'submerged' lost talent of the world and helped it 'fit in' with human pity, human progress, making its possessions not alone respectable but self-respecting.

"And, put this to his eternal credit, he was the Optimist of Salvation. Moreover, he taught, and the lesson sometimes needs exposition, financial caution to the disordered enthusiasms of unthinking charity. Believing in himself he conquered the world's disbelief. Knowing full well how surely mankind is born to duties rather than to rights, he taught and practiced duty; and, putting his hand to the plough, never swerved from the straight furrow, though often the way was long and the soil implacable" (Aug. 22).

In America, newspaper editorialists were equally magnanimous. The New York *Morning Telegraph* called him "the Wesley of the nineteenth century" and suggested that he deserved to be buried in Westminster Abbey. "No man of his time," wrote the editor of the New York *Times*, "did more for the benefit of the people than William Booth. He placed charity on a practical basis. He taught religion to the lowliest in terms which they could comprehend. Cleanliness, decency, and the will to do good thrived under his rule" (Aug. 21).

## A PATRIARCH

The New York *Sun* added: "General Booth was a patriarch. He had that quality of mind that made the maintenance of discipline over his heterogeneous followers possible. Without that capacity for leadership he would have been an exhorter, a revivalist, but never the head of a body that embraced within its ranks impassioned orators, acute businessmen, artisans and laborers, all devoting their energies and their gifts to a common purpose, with common enthusiasm and self-denial" (Aug. 21).

In a similar vein, the Seattle *Republican* reiterated the common tribute of praise in nearly every American newspaper. "History fails to record any person," it commented, "who did as much for fallen humanity as did General William Booth during his lifetime, and his recent passing but wound up his personal career on earth and made it possible for him to use his passport to that 'home not made by hands, eternal in the heavens. Though his remains now be but a lump of lifeless clay, not his soul, but his good examples and his work will live on and go on almost as if he were directing them.

"That the world is a million times better that General Booth lived no one will deny and the human being was not living, who did not drop a tear of regret, on hearing of his death. He was without religious creed or doctrine, but was full and overflowing with the love of God and right and justice toward his fellow man, and that was worth more than all of the creeds and isms ascribed to Christianity. The civilized world will pay homage to his memory one day next week and a more befitting tribute could not be paid to the memory of a life so nobly spent" (Aug. 23).

"Take him all for all," wrote the editor of the Toronto *Globe and Mail,* "William Booth was among the first ten of the world's great men of the past two decades. In certain elements of greatness he stood alone. With none of the advantages of social prestige or of financial aid or of rare intellectual power, he accomplished in his lifetime a task of such world magnitude as commanded not recognition alone, but sincere personal admiration from three British sovereigns, and won the reverent affection of an innumerable host out of every nation of mankind.

"And he did it by the masterful power of a great idea. His life was truth vitalized and made redemptive . . . No man believed more terrifically in the sinfulness of sin and in its inevitable penalty. No man believed more unalteringly in the essential worthiness of life's waifs and strays. No one relied more implicitly on the Power that is not man's power. The measure of the prodigal's torment was to him the measure of the prodigal's worth, and with the dauntless optimism of his faith he 'never turned his back, but marched breast forward.' A king among men, so long as the world counts" (Aug. 21).

## RELIGIOUS EULOGIES

The religious papers were especially gracious in their expressions of condolence. The New York *Christian Advocate* credited the General with "the happiest blend of spiritual fervor and social enthusiasm known to the world since the days of John Wesley," while the Boston *Congregationalist,* putting aside any kind of comparison, simply ranked him on a plane with "the greatest philanthropists and Christians of all times," adding that he belonged in the company of such great men as Dwight L. Moody, John Wesley, George Fox, Cromwell, Luther, Loyola, Peter and Paul.

And, finally, *The Northwestern Christian Advocate* offered this key to the Army's success: "Those who insist on war as necessary to furnish a motive for heroic action could well study the spiritual analog as exemplified in the life and works of this great man. What more thrilling than to battle with iniquity, following it to its lair in the city's slum and destroying it with the weapons of spiritual warfare?" It concluded with this prediction: "A great man has fallen. His work will march on."

What is impressive about the preceding tributes is not only that nearly all were magnanimous in the words of praise, but that each of them had something slightly different to say about Booth's life and accomplishments. There were just a few newspapers—a very few—who either chose not to join the flood of approbation (many Catholic journals being conspicuous among them) or decided they would not suddenly change their opinion about the Salvation Army. *The Saturday Review,* for example, which had always been (since the early 1880s) an outspoken critic of the Army, and of Booth in particular, wrote of his death in a shrugging sort of way:

> *Another—perhaps the last—of the big Victorians gone. His blood and thunder evangelism tailed off into an enormous "business proposition" out harroding Harrods. As for his accomplishments, they would prove transitory: When Booth discovered that "it is of little use to preach Gospel to a man who wants a loaf; we must give him a loaf first," it was inevitable, in modern days, that the business of loaf-providing would gradually swallow up the evangelization. He will leave no great religious movement behind him, as Wesley did. His social schemes are proving failures. What William Booth did was to create a temporary stirring of foul and stagnating waters by means of transient religious commotion (Aug 24).*

## OLD WOUNDS

Across the ocean, the New York *Times,* though quite generous in its editorial praise, tried to open old wounds by speculating whether William Booth's death might bring Ballington Booth and his Volunteers back into the Army fold. Reviving the 1896 controversy, the *Times* chose at that moment to reprint a full-page article titled "Ballington Booth's Suppressed Farewell Letter" saying that "it was inevitable that the death of General William Booth should reopen the discussion, now 16 years old, concerning the breach between himself and his son, Ballington, which resulted in a schism in the Salvation Army, and commenced a family dissension which, contrary to all expectations, not even the death of the veteran evangelist has put an end to" (Aug. 22).

This attempt, on the part of the New York *Times,* to renew the controversy did not attract much attention in any quarter. All that a few other newspapers did was to print a statement by Ballington Booth, denying that any members of the Salvation Army had attempted a reconciliation and deploring any attempt by any newspaper to revive the regretful incident. He had, he said, only a desire to remain silent, except to say that he had always treated his father with the deference due a great man and that he had written "with affectionate solicitude" to his brother, Bramwell.

Only one note of bitterness crept in: "His youngest brother and second sister are out of the Army, and he [Ballington] has no knowledge of any effort being made within these last days or at any time towards reconciliation. He would have gone to his sister, Eva, but when he and his brother, Herbert, attempted to offer their sympathies at the time of Mrs. Booth-Tucker's death [in 1903], they were met with rebuff" (Toronto *Globe and Mail, Aug. 22).*

That was the only—by and large an unnoticed—sour note in the outpouring of public sympathy. Most editorialists were kind, and though some still did not approve of Salvation Army methods (and said so), they were all in agreement regarding the personal integrity and the historical importance of the man who had just died.

## MIRACLE WORKER

The *South African News* summed it up best: "William Booth is dead. And with him passed away one of the most vivid and most striking personalities the world has ever seen. Rough and rugged, it dominated an empire which is like no other empire—a spiritual empire, unique among such, held by an army whose motto is 'Blood and Fire,' whose weapon is the tambourine, and whose battle-cry is 'Hallelujah!' . . .

"As an achievement, the Army is a miracle wrought in an age of materialism, of so outstanding and so striking a nature that, even if it ceased tomorrow, the name of the man who worked it must endure. You may disagree with the methods of the Army; you may even think its tactics reprehensible; but you must recognize the miracle and acknowledge the gifts of the miracle worker" (Aug. 22).

On Sunday, August 25, the church pulpits echoed the newspaper sentiments. At St. Paul's Cathedral, Canon Newbolt "said that the commanding genius, the resolute determination, and unsparing devotion of William Booth had forced their way to the front of public opinion, in spite of obloquy and sometimes of opposition. William Booth had firmly laid hold of the great truth, from which he never swerved, that to raise submerged man one must deal with his spiritual as well as his bodily and mental condition.

"Salvation was a permanent idea in his scheme, which a materialistic age might do well to notice while it praised what was noble in the man and enthusiastic in his work. A religious and benevolent life, such as that of William Booth, still had power to excite the approbation of men and lift them up from things temporal to things eternal" (*Times*, Aug. 26).

At Regent's Park Baptist Chapel, the Reverend F.B. Meyer contrasted the beginning of the Salvation Army with the honor now being bestowed on its General: "Every conceivable obstacle that physical violence, ridicule, sarcasm and slander could put in his way was overcome. By the help of the Almighty he built a bridge over which multitudes have passed from despair to hope, from the edge of the pit to the threshold of Heaven."

## NO SOUL LOST

The Reverend Wilson Carlile, founder of The Church Army, preaching at Totland Bay, on the Isle of Wight, called Booth one of the world's greatest evangelists; the Reverend Archibald of the Church of Scotland suggested that Booth's distinctive message was that there need be no such thing as "waste humanity" and, stripped of all its distractions, that was essential Salvationism, so wonderfully near Christ.

Even Father McKenna, preaching in the Roman Catholic Cathedral at Westminster, though regretting that Booth had not taught the "whole doctrine of the Catholic Church," nevertheless admitted that "in one or two points" he had imitated his Master more nearly than many another Christian minister, "for by his street preaching and in his near approach to the lowest stratum of mankind 'General' Booth made use of weapons which had been left to rust by other Christian Churches" (*Times*, Aug. 26).

At most Salvation Army corps, the Sunday following Booth's death was a somber one and though the open-air services were still held and the music blared as loudly (because Booth would have wanted that) there was an air of solemnity to it all. Here is how a reporter from *The Westminster Gazette* described his "Impressions of Sunday with the Salvationists":

There was something strangely moving about the Sunday processions of the Salvation Army corps yesterday morning. It was the usual program—singing, drumming, trumpeting; and wherever they came to a standstill in the streets of the poor suburban districts, the same sequence of prayer and music and exhortation. But somehow it was not the same. How could it be, when, at least in the hearts and minds of the officers and soldiers, there must have been the thought that this was their General's "first Sunday in Heaven"?

They wore the same uniforms, without a sign of mourning, and their voices and brass instruments rang as cheerfully as ever. Only, somehow, there was a touch of solemnity and of a deeper emotion added to the open-air services, which sent a hush all along the streets, and seemed to attract people almost in spite of themselves.

## Irresistible Force

The loud-voiced young woman, in ulsters frayed at the hem and torn at the greasy pockets, who stood about, evidently "out for a lark," might try to brazen out the preachers and musicians, but one by one they were silenced, and drawn as if by some irresistible force towards the circle on the center of the road, over which the Salvation Army flag floated. It would be difficult to say whether, having come to scoff, they remained to pray, but they certainly stood by with their rough red hands folded, and their faces very quiet.

The more "respectable" part of the community, who as a rule consider it not quite genteel to pay attention to the Army, paused a moment as they passed, and not a few men lifted their hats, in token of respect for the dead leader. Lads in their teens, as a rule absolutely superior to any emotional influences, stood leaning against the houses and rather shamefacedly watching the men who stood bare-headed, praying to the "God of the Army, the Father of the Poor, the help of the helpless" that He might guide them still, and make them more zealous to save souls, now that their leader was no longer with them in the flesh.

And gradually, as one beautiful and popular hymn after the other was played and sung, the crowd around the Salvationists thickened, and many an offering, given by those who can but offer little, was quietly put into the collecting box which the Hallelujah Lass, as usual, carried round. There was no extra commotion, no special appeal to attention, in the Sunday street services, but when the little band marched on, to the tune of that hymn which at least the present generation will never hear without a special thrill, "Nearer my God to Thee," the noisy street became as silent as a cathedral, and there was not a face but had upon it the look that only comes when the heart and the spirit are stirred to the depths (Aug. 26).

Probably no greater tribute could have been paid: that men and women should pause and listen to the Army's message; that men should doff their hats as a token of respect for the dead leader; that common people should share in the common soldiers' grief.

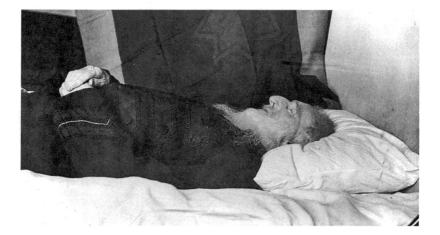

*"From as early as 5:00 a.m. until 10 p.m., two continuous streams of people passed by on either side of the catafalque."*

## CHAPTER FOUR

# Lying-in-State

Shortly before midnight on Thursday, August 22, the body of General Booth was driven by his grandson, Bernard, to the Clapton Congress Hall where it would lie "in state" for public viewing. Originally the duration of the "lying-in-state" had been scheduled for two days (Friday and Saturday), but public demand necessitated an extension to four (Monday and Tuesday as well), for on the first day alone more than fifty thousand people passed by the glass-covered coffin.

There was nothing dark or depressing in what they saw. "The interior of the Clapton Congress Hall," wrote a *Times* reporter, "was more cheerful than the dismal, rain-swept streets outside. On entering the place one was impressed by the brightness of it all. The strong rays of electric light beat down upon the deep rich hues of the Salvationist flags, which were arranged around the great hall.

"The platform and the space in front of it blazed with color, for here, where the General lay, there were none of the conventional trappings of woe. No black draperies were permitted to approach the body of the Army's commander. The signs of mourning were the touches of white here and there among the banners and the white armlets worn by members of the guard and the officers who were on duty about the coffin" (Aug. 24).

Under a lofty canopy of yellow and white, the plain pine coffin rested on a marble catafalque [ornamental structure]. "The foot of the coffin was covered with Army colors, and across the upper portion, above the glass panel which revealed the face and shoulders of the dead leader, was folded that famous flag which he carried to Calvary on his visit to Palestine seven years ago. Upon the flag were the familiar peaked cap, the Bible and hymnbook, and the fountain pen—an inseparable companion—in its red leather case. Behind the coffin was displayed the portrait of Mrs. Booth, which for many years had hung in the General's study. Around and about were palms and green shrubs. Beyond the catafalque rose the platform, and in the center two Salvationist lassies supported a large framed photograph of the General" [*Times, Aug. 24*].

An honor-guard composed mainly of male and female officer-cadets surrounded the coffin—standing silently, with bowed heads, two at the head of the coffin, one on either side and one at the foot—each holding a Salvation Army flag. The whole spectacle was impressive and inspiring and came under the oversight of Colonel Fred Cox, who had been for many years General Booth's private secretary, who now lovingly attended to the details of the funeral arrangements.

"All the time," his biographer writes, "he was filled with a sense of personal responsibility to guard the casket with its precious contents. His figure stands out in the memory of thousands who passed through the Congress Hall. He was struck by the large number of officers and others who brought handkerchiefs to him and asked him, 'Just to wipe the glass lid' of the coffin that they might have a personal remembrance.

## CONTINUOUS STREAMS

Throughout the long hours of each day—from as early as five o'clock in the morning until ten at night—"two continuous streams of people passed through the barriers on either side of the catafalque." The barriers themselves, covered with crimson cloth, added to the blaze of color and so slowly was each person allowed to proceed that everyone had time to pause for a moment and gaze on the figure within the coffin.

"What they saw was just the General as many of them had known him in life. The blue frock coat and the crimson jersey were a homely familiar spectacle. The thin white hands were crossed upon the breast. The face was the color of delicate yellow ivory, and the aquiline nose, the white hair, and the flowing white beard presented the patriarchal appearance, which was so characteristic of the General in later years. The eyes were closed, and the expression of the face was one of dignified calm, just as though the General were quietly asleep.

"It was a reverent throng that passed by the coffin. Outward signs of grief were infrequent, and in fact would have appeared rather out of place amid such surroundings. But the faces of the people betokened sympathy and quiet regret. All classes were represented—laboring men and women, costers [fruit-and-vegetable vendors], flower girls, policemen, cab-drivers, business and professional men, soldiers and sailors, clerks and tradesmen, clergymen and ministers. The East-end workers, among whom the Army had its beginnings, were strongly represented. One coster came up to an officer and said he was a 'deputation' from a number of 'mates' who wished to send a wreath. 'We want it laid on the coffin of the General,' he said, 'him wot's gone to Heaven, worse luck!'" [*Times*, Aug. 24].

That wreath, like most, was sent to the International Headquarters on Queen Victoria Street, for Bramwell Booth had decided there would be no flowers present at the lying-in-state.

## A FOUR-FOOT WREATH

There were a very few exceptions, of course. For it would have been an impertinence beyond belief to have rejected the magnificent four-foot floral wreath sent by the British King and Queen on the afternoon of the 26th. Delivered by Lieutenant-Colonel Powley of the Lord Chamberlain's Office, the wreath, composed of "trumpet lilies, orchids, and lilies of the valley" encased in palm leaves, was placed at the head of the coffin.

When it was announced that the wreath was from the King and Queen, and "God Save the King" was sung, the people present in the hall responded with a loud "Amen." It was also of special significance to Bramwell Booth that Queen Alexandra sent her own personal bouquet of flowers. She had been a special friend of the Army and her wreath, composed of "lilies, orchids and stephanotis" was placed next to that of the official royal offering.

There were but a few interruptions to the flow of viewers, such as when those wreaths and that of the Kaiser were delivered, and when the family members themselves attended the viewing early on the second morning. "At half past nine," reported the *Daily Express,* "the hall was cleared for the visit of Commissioner Lucy Booth, the late General's third daughter, and others of the family. Nine grandchildren, including two sons and two daughters of General and Mrs. Bramwell Booth, and five children of Commander Booth-Tucker, passed by the coffin. Then came Mrs. Booth-Hellberg and her children, and the child of Mrs. Booth-Clibborn.

"Mrs. Booth-Hellberg is the head of the Army in Denmark, and had not seen her father for some years until his last illness. She fell on her knees beside the coffin for a moment's prayer, and as she rose to her feet some sudden inspiration set the people singing the opening verse of a favorite Salvation hymn:

> All I have I am bringing to Thee,
> In Thy steps I will follow,
> Come joy or come sorrow,
> My Jesus I will follow Thee.

"All the members of the family joined in, and even the twelve officers on guard raised their eyes from the ground and started singing too in a manner as unlike the conventional idea of any scene of death, as it was characteristic of Salvation Army methods" [August 26].

Other than those few interruptions, the whole "lying-in-state" was of a quiet nature. As more than a hundred thousand people took their silent farewell of the General, an orchestra played softly the familiar Army hymns, or a "sweet-toned" choir sang the refrains which the General loved—'Sweeping through the gates of the new Jerusalem,' 'When the roll is called up yonder' and many others.

## CHILDREN OF POVERTY

It was a cosmopolitan crowd that slowly made its way past the coffin. "I watched," wrote Philip Gibbs, "part of the almost endless procession of men and women who came to this lying-in-state, and the memory of it will linger with me. This was a pilgrimage from the mean streets of the great city. Illustrious personages had sent wreaths and tributes, now and again a carriage stood outside the hall, but for the most part those who came to get one moment's glimpse of the old General's face were the children of poverty. Here were working men in their working clothes, and the women of humble life—those people who live always on a thin crust above the abyss, and who need great courage, great strength of character, great luck to prevent themselves from falling through.

"There were poor clerks, and down-at-heel fellows of shabby gentility, and out-of-works who have been into many an Army 'shelter' on a winter's night, and poor devils who still look to the Army for something hot to drink, and something to ease the hunger pains. The instinct of loyalty, a genuine love for 'the old man,' a remembrance, perhaps, of some moment of rare emotion when their horny hands clutched up to God, had brought them, perhaps, at the risk of losing a day's job, to his bier.

"There was no unrestrained emotionalism. Only by the quiver of a lip, by a moist eye, by a queer scared look on a rugged face, did one see that these people were moved profoundly. But it was a great and solemn sight, and men like myself, the lookers-on of life, the critics, the reporters, who have not been followers of the general's flag, who follow, perhaps, other flags, or none at all, saw here the testimony to General Booth's greatness and the victory of his life. He had been the friend of humanity, the lover of those who had 'gone under,' and of all who suffer and sin. Now that he lay dead they did not forget" [*The Graphic*, Aug. 31].

## DEVOTIONAL SERVICE

On the last day of the "lying-in-state," while a long queue waited outside Clapton Congress Hall, a devotional service, conducted by Commissioner McKie, was held for the nearly 400 hundred cadets and staff of the Army's Training College. After the day's viewing was over, and the crowds around the hall had diminished, the coffin containing the General's body, preceded by his flag, was placed in a motor-hearse and, accompanied by Commissioner Sturgess, in charge of the Army's social work, by Commissioner Railton, Major Dean and Brigadier Aspinall, was taken to the Olympia for the next night's memorial service.

In a symbolic gesture, the route chosen was through Whitechapel, past the original headquarters of the Army, past the

Mansion House to the new headquarters on Queen Victoria Street ("where a momentary halt was made"), and thence along the Embankment to the Olympia. All along the route, though late at night, people lined up to reverently salute the passing cortege as it made its way on yet another stage of its journey to Abney Park.

*"Go straight for souls, and go for the worst."*

## CHAPTER FIVE

# A Service of Celebration

Covering four acres of ground in West Kensington, the Olympia was the largest exhibition hall in England, and on Wednesday evening, August 28, it was filled to capacity as more than 25,000 Salvationists and friends gathered to say "farewell" to their dead General. So large was the assembly and so vast the arena—so certain was it that it would be impossible "to address the audience with any hope of being heard by those who are any considerable distance from the speaker"—that it was necessary to script the whole performance in a fifty-one page program. Thus, by closely observing the number displayed from the platform and by following the instructions for that number, everyone would know what was happening and be able to participate.

## ELECTRIFYING HARMONY

Thus, though most of the audience might not hear the first song being announced, they could see the large "No. 2" being displayed, then rise to their feet (as the program requested) and sing "There is a better world, they say, Oh, so bright! / Where sin and woe are done away, Oh, so bright!" With 25,000 voices blended in harmony, the effect was, as the reporters averred, electrifying. And so, through the long program, even through to the "appeal" which featured William Booth's own entreaties (#20–28), the choreographed service was both impressive and spiritually uplifting. Here is how a reporter for *The Daily Chronicle* so eloquently described it:

> [It seemed] a strange place in which to honor the dust of a great hero, and one in which a strange memory was revived. Here, under the glass roof, was, not long ago, the cathedral scene of Reinhardt's mystery play, "The Miracle." That was wonderful in its religious emotion, in its great appeal to the spiritual heart of humanity. But last night here was a miracle play more wonderful, because it was no make believe, but a reality of modern life.
>
> This religious emotion was no actor's counterfeit. These tears came from men and women grief stricken with the loss of a great leader. The spiritual flame, which burned in this great congregation, was lighted in the streets and slums of modern cities by the enkindling fire of one man's genius. And there in the coffin was the Miracle itself—the dead body of the frail old man, who in life had, by faith, by courage, by sublime endeavor, formed a worldwide army devoted to the service of God and man, and who, in death, will still call them onwards to duty by the undying power of his personality.
>
> The scene was astounding and beautiful as a tribute to this great Christian and soldier of the Lord. Battalion after battalion of the old general's troops marched into the hall until the whole of the arena was the camping ground of this vast army, arranged in orderly detachments.
>
> Bright lights burned above them, but no single face was visible among the multitude below the platform, only the white, vague

*blur of innumerable faces, thousands of them deeply shadowed be-*
*low the poke-bonnets of the women officers, thousands of them*
*bowed in prayer. For an hour or more, there had been the steady*
*tramp of feet, down below on the floor space, and high up in the*
*galleries, like the sound of muffled drums. Above the platform, tier*
*above tier, were the white frocks of the Army's children, and a le-*
*gion of little faces peering down. In the center of the great platform*
*there was a glare of scarlet and gold where the united bands were*
*massed.*

*Below and all around the platform there were the wreaths of*
*victory sent by many great people of the world for a hero's burial.*
*Their scent rose as an incense about the place where his body was*
*about to rest. At the far end of the long highway of this amphithe-*
*atre, and pointing upwards to the dome, there were the Army's*
*standards, draped not in black, but in white ribbons, each one a flag*
*of honor borne on many a field of battle (Aug. 29).*

When the vast audience had been assembled, the most
solemn moment of the service began. Punctually at 7:30, the
united bands played a verse to the tune "Better World" and the
25,000 rose as a single person, and sang the well-loved song.
Then the funeral procession entered the hall to the magnificent
strains of Handel's "Dead March in Saul."

"A more impressive scene has probably never been witnessed
in our generation," wrote a reporter for *The Daily Mirror.* "Veteran
soldiers, clad in the Army's uniform, walked in the van. Captains,
majors, brigadiers, colonels, commissioners, and their wives,
officers from other lands, moved slowly down the center of the
hall . . . The first flags carried in the *cortege* were draped with
white ribbons. Some of the women in the ranks were weeping,
but the general air was one of calm and reverential dignity. The
flash of color, and the blue and scarlet banners were the more
dazzling by contrast with the somber garb of the dense multitudes in the arena" [Aug. 23].

Then came the most solemn moment. The General's "Calvary
Flag'" carried by Brigadier Fred Cox preceded the carriage which
contained the plain pine coffin covered with an Army flag on

which rested the General's Bible and cap. In the hushed auditorium, the stillness broken only by an occasional sob, the cortege made its way slowly to the front. "It was," a reporter commented, "an indescribably thrilling moment:

'Lo! The leader in these glorious wars, Now to glorious burial slowly borne'!"

## A CURIOUS WHISPER

Behind the coffin, came the Booth family: General Bramwell and his wife, Florence, followed by Commissioner Eva, Commissioner Lucy Booth-Hellberg, Catherine Booth-Clibborn, Herbert and several grandchildren, among them: Adj. Catherine Booth, Captain Mary Booth, Captain Miriam Booth, Sergeant Bernard Booth and Cadet Motee-BoothTucker.

As the small procession made its way slowly up the center aisle, the immense audience remained standing and all the Salvation Army soldiers gave the distinctive Army salute (arm raised and index finger pointing to Heaven) as it passed. "It was as though," wrote one reporter, "the spirit of General Booth passed also, with a benediction upon those bowed heads, and with quiet words that plucked at the heart strings, and touched them to the soul. There was no noise of grief. There were no hysterical outbursts of emotion. But thousands of men and women were in tears, and as step by step the bier went slowly on, one heard, very faintly, a curious kind of whisper, which was the deep-drawn sigh of a great crowd" [*Graphic*, Aug. 29].

For some of those who attended—the King's equerry, several mayors in their robes and chains of office, ministers and clergymen from all the Protestant churches, and two Jewish rabbis (all seated in the front rows)—this must have seemed a most unusual funeral service. But for most of those assembled—including the several thousand banked around the outskirts of the hall—what followed was not merely a "memorial" service but a mammoth meeting of prayer and praise.

## SPIRIT OF THE ARMY

"It was," continued the *Graphic* reporter, "one of the greatest victories of simple faith and of religious organization which the modern world has seen. The spirit of the Salvation Army—with its discipline, its ordered emotion, its training in devotion, in prayer, in choral singing—was seen at its best. Very few words were spoken, and those were inaudible to most of the individuals in that multitude. But by great numbers held up at every stage of the service, and corresponding to the service book which was in each hand, immense and startling effects were produced, building up to a great edifice of disciplined fervor. Tremendous was the volume of sound, which filled the hall and swept up to the dome in rising waves, when the hymns were sung by thousands of voices in perfect unison.

> When the roll is called in Heaven
> And the host shall muster there,
> I will take my place among them
> And their joys and triumphs share.

"Those people did not sing from their throats alone, but from their hearts. There was in this thrill of the voice, in this ardor of sound, the spirit of men and women who have sung in haunts of misery, in the quarters of despair, on the battlefields of vice and crime. When they sang the General's own hymn—O boundless salvation, deep ocean of love—they seemed as though once more they saw the figure of the old General himself, beating time, raising his arms, singing in his hoarse whisper, with the melody in his eyes and the joy of the words illumining his face.

"But if the hymns were impressive, the silences were still more affecting. At given moments the big figures were held up on the platform, and there followed long, unearthly silences, unbroken by any cough, by any shuffling of feet, by any of that restlessness and murmuring which is to be heard in the stillness of any crowd. This hush was like that of death itself.

"During these spells of silence the people read pages of the service book, in which the general's words spoke to them as often in life. Here were his messages of faith, of honor, of love, of duty, of self-sacrifice—the spirit which he poured into his own work, and by which he achieved his victories."

## Promise of Allegiance

"It was a wonderful manifestation of the spiritual emotion that still underlies modern life, and of the great hunger of the human soul for religious comfort and for an ideal above material desires. Above the coffin the music sang of new victories. This memorial service to General Booth was not a farewell only, but a promise of allegiance in the days to come to the flag of the Salvation Army, with which his spirit will go marching on.

"The culmination of this meeting, as had been the culmination of nearly every meeting William Booth had conducted, was an 'invitation to salvation.' After the main service—the songs, prayers, a special song by a children's choir—the congregation read silently several extracts from William Booth's writings, the readings being interspersed by hymns, after which the invitation was given to 'backsliders and sinners,' to come to the 'Mercy Seat.'

"While thousands sang 'Come, Sinner, Come!' dozens of persons forced their way through the crowded aisles to the mercy seats on either side of the platform, where they knelt beside the officers who had been selected to receive them . . . Striding back and forth on the platform, General Bramwell Booth, swinging his arms above his head, led the singing, pausing frequently to remind sinners that the dead leader had given his life to saving them . . . The revival service was concluded with the singing of the refrain heard at every meeting which General Booth conducted, 'His blood can make the vilest clean; His blood avails for me.' All the soldiers of the Army rose and recited the Covenant of Fidelity, pledging themselves to be faithful soldiers of the Lord" [Globe and Mail, Aug. 29].

"Never," wrote the reporter for The Daily Graphic, "has the militarism of the Salvation Army been put before us with such living evidence as it was last night at Olympia. It was a wonderful congregation, impressive in its immensity . . . It had no thought for the ritual of sorrow. It sang lustily with a cheerful voice in the presence of its dead leader; and throughout the service the dominating note was one of sturdy confidence and happy resolution rather than one of regret or lamentation.

"Then a few simple sentences came out from Commissioner Lawley's prayer, and we began to understand. He prayed in a voice of extraordinary volume, and he delivered up thanks to the Creator for 'triumph in the battle, for faith in the darkness.' And then, as the bearded Commissioner cried out, 'We praise Thee for victory in death,' those who were strangers looked up and realized that here was a victorious army celebrating the greatest of triumphs, and not a retinue of sad-eyed mourners weeping for the dead."

*Commissioner John Lawley (L) and Bramwell Booth, the new General (R)*

## CHAPTER SIX

# "We Are an Army!"

"General Booth made his last march yesterday," reported the London *Daily Express*, "with 6,000 soldiers before him. It was a march of triumph. The somber spirit of death that stalks in the funerals of most great men had no place in this mile-long stream of soldiers. They went their way with white pennants fluttering gaily in the wind, the captured flags of the nations carried proudly before them. And the cemetery before them they swept through the gates to a conquered land" [Aug. 30].

That was the common perception of William Booth's funeral march and the funeral itself. "A man must be dull of soul," ventured the London *Times*, "who is unimpressed by what took place yesterday in London, when the Salvation Army laid the remains of their dead Chief to rest. For it was a rare and singular thing." And the *Daily Mirror* claimed that "the scene was more of triumph rather than defeat, for whilst the Salvationists mourned the loss of the General their demeanor spoke of rejoicing at his promotion to a more exalted service."

The tone of amazement stemmed partly from the fact that a man of such humble beginnings should have won for himself such a "tribute of devotion." For, not only were there 6,000 Salvationists in the triumphal march, but probably twice that many in the nearly two million people who crowded the thoroughfares which the cortege passed through. They were from all walks of life, many of the important personages having claimed the balconies which lined the streets, but below them were "the factory girls, laborers, hawkers, navvies," many of the East End workers to whom Booth had preached.

"Here is a poor mother with her children, 'The Salvation Army has done a lot for me: she says. 'The General was a real friend to us.' A strange funeral! Every soul in these poor streets seemed to regard the General as their own friend, and even now that he was dead they were easy and familiar with him—just as they would rally him at one of his famous meetings . . . To be all things to all men—was not that the secret of it? Love alone, let us believe, prompted him to his work, made him a missionary amongst them. Love, too, came back to him many thousand-fold in those multitudes gathered to take leave" [*Daily Mirror,* Aug. 30].

But the amazement derived also from the Army's declared resolve to "celebrate" their dead leader's life and accomplishments and to admit no "trappings of woe." The most striking note in "the remarkable procession and ceremony," continued the *Times,* "was the air of gladness pervading the ranks of the Army . . . It would not be true to say that there has been no woe or no mourning, but the sign of mourning has been white, and the bearing of the mourners has been glad and proud.

"They are undismayed by the death of their Chief, the father of the family. This is one of the things they have learnt from him, and it is one of the secrets of his influence . . . It is very noteworthy that so many men and women should be imbued with this spirit of confidence and cheerfulness. It surrounds them with an atmosphere of serenity and happiness peculiarly valuable, and indeed essential to their work. They derive it from the inspiration of their leader—from his personality and intense faith."

## SEVEN THOUSAND STRONG

The funeral procession itself was, as William Booth would have had it, as much a show of strength, a display of Salvation Army resolve, as it was a march of honor. To the nearly two million people who lined the streets of London, sometimes twenty deep along the pavements, this was a statement of intention—to carry on William Booth's ministry of mercy as he had intended The Salvation Army always should. It was a spectacle dignified yet impressive, one seldom witnessed on the streets of London, and few who did could mistake its purpose.

At approximately 10:45 a.m. on that Thursday morning nearly seven thousand Salvationists from across Britain and from many countries around the world gathered on the Embankment to be organized into "Brigades"—thirty-eight of them comprising officers and delegates from various divisions interspersed by thirteen brass band combinations. "Two-thirds of the processionists," wrote a reporter for *The Christian World,* "were women, and it was pitiful to see them drenched in spite of their umbrellas, many of them had not even that protection" [Sept. 5]. There were fifty-one brigades in all, the members being arranged six abreast behind their flags. Interspersed between every third or fourth brigade were three brass bands (about forty in all), arranged so that while one played the "Dead March" the other two remained silent. By this arrangement it was possible to keep an unbroken sound of music to which the procession slowly marched.

By the time the procession started, at precisely half-past eleven, the rain had ceased and the sun shone brightly. The first Brigade consisted of foreign officers carrying the flags of heir respective countries, followed by the Clapton Congress Hall, Bristol I and Cradley Heath bands. And so the arrangement continued:

three or four brigades of officers, interspersed by bands from various corps, until Brigade 47, which was composed of the Chalk Farm, Regent Hall, and International Staff Bands, followed immediately by Brigade 48 which would, at the International Headquarters, become the funeral cortege. When drawn up, before setting off, the funeral procession stretched along the Embankment from Charing Cross to Blackfriars Bridge, a distance of one and a half miles.

## SIMPLICITY

The funeral cortege itself and the coffin (in an open carriage drawn by "two fine chestnut horses") reposed just outside the International Headquarters at 101 Victoria Street where the Salvation Army flag was at full mast, signifying victory. Draped over the coffin was the flag which General Booth had raised on Mount Calvary during his visit in 1905, upon which were placed his cap and his Bible.

"At each corner of the coffin was another Army flag upright, and at the sides were tall palms. In front of the car was an open carriage filled with magnificent red and white blooms—the wreaths of the King (George V), the German Emperor, and of other sympathizers. But there were no flowers upon the coffin, nothing to hide the severe simplicity of the Army emblem which was dear to the Army's founder" [Times, Aug. 30].

As the procession passed the coffin, at about 12:30 p.m. (an hour after having left the Embankment) the dead General received the salute of the Salvationists who marched in it. As each Brigade approached, their flags were lowered, the men's caps doffed, the bands played the "Dead March" from Handel's *Saul,* and every officer and soldier turned reverently towards the coffin and gravely saluted the dead leader.

When Brigade 47 had passed the solemn saluting point, the remaining portion of the procession halted while the car containing the coffin and the carriage in which were the wreaths took their place in the ranks. Immediately behind the coffin "General" Bramwell and Mrs. Booth walked. He wore a blue cloak lined with red, and she had a sash of white and red across her jacket.

The other members of the family followed the new "General" and his wife, and behind them came the commissioners, colonels, and lieutenant-colonels with their wives. In this group, which immediately preceded the International Headquarters Staff, were some of the late General's oldest friends and comrades.

## EVA BOOTH

But perhaps the happiest to be there, though the saddest as well, was Commissioner Evangeline Booth who, by sheer good luck (the grace of God, she said), had reached London just the day before. The *Daily Mail* told the story of her experience:

"Few who saw Miss Eva Booth, the daughter of the late General and Chief Commissioner of the Salvation Army in America, at her father's funeral yesterday realized what she had gone through to be in time to take a last farewell of her parent. "Kiss him for me," Miss Booth cabled from New York when she was apprised last week of the death of the General.

"But by an achievement in Atlantic travel she was able to kiss her father with her own lips before the funeral ceremony took place. When she received the sad news Miss Booth determined to make an attempt to reach London in time for her father's funeral. Enormous difficulties confronted her. At the onset she found she had but one hour in which to catch the first boat to Europe.

"That one hour, however, was enough, and she succeeded in boarding the French liner "La France" just before the boat steamed out of New York Harbor.

"But her difficulties were by no means over. She could not come directly to England in that boat.

"'La France' reached Havre on Wednesday evening. Here again fortune favored Miss Booth.

"An express train was just leaving for Paris. She caught it with thirty seconds to spare.

"Paris reached, Miss Booth took the first available train back to the coast—to Calais. Here she boarded the cross-channel steamer and crossed to Dover.

"From Dover as fast as the first train could bring her to London, ultimately reaching Charing Cross Station at 5:40 yesterday morning."

After the funeral cortege had joined the procession, the Salvationists, with their bands now playing more spirited tunes, slowly made their way along Queen Victoria Street, Mansion House Street, Cornhill, Leadenhall Street, St. Mary Axe, Camomile Street, Bishopsgate, Norton Folgate, Kingsland Road, Kingsland High Street, Stoke Newington Road, Stoke Newington High Street to Abney Park Cemetery. Over five miles altogether.

## RESPECT AND REVERENCE

"From beginning to end," wrote the reporter from the *Daily Chronicle,* "it was a triumphal procession . . . All down the great line the familiar banners of the Army waved like oriflames of war. City thoroughfares were packed from end to end, and every high window was occupied by spectators. Businessmen had deserted their desks, and clerks had forsaken their stools. All business seemed to be suspended, and on every side were 46 signs of respect and reverence for this religious leader.

"Flags were flown at half-mast, and on the balcony of the Mansion House the Lord Mayor's deputy (the Lord Mayor being out of town) stood in his robes and chain of office, surrounded by members of the City Corporation and officials, and saluted as the hearse passed. On the roof of the Bank of England, on the steps of the Royal Exchange and of the Baltic in St. Mary—axe businessmen watched the great pageant go by."

At approximately three o'clock, by which time the sun was shining brightly, the long procession reached Abney Park Cemetery just off the Stoke Newington High Street. As it passed through the boroughs of Hackney and Stoke Newington, "people of all classes were as eager to do reverence to the dead as were those in the City [of London], and the mayors of both boroughs attended in state at the cemetery gates. Within a short distance a banner spread across High Street bore the words "The Metropolitan Boroughs of Hackney and Stoke Newington mourn the loss of a noble life."

The marshaling of the fifty-one brigades inside the cemetery took nearly an hour. After the long march, many Salvationists collapsed, men and women fainting in the bright sun. Bars of chocolate were distributed to those who suffered from fatigue. "So thickly were the mourners packed about the grave," the *Daily Mirror* reported, "that there seemed to be a constant stream of fainting people being carried away."

## LAID TO REST

At precisely 4 p.m., however, in that southwestern corner of the "nonconformist" cemetery—"in a quiet corner over-shadowed by lofty trees" and overlooked by the statue of Isaac Watts— William Booth was finally laid to rest. There the Salvation Army had already reserved some burial plots and, indeed, it was a spot already enshrined (in the minds of Salvationists) as being the burial site of the General's wife, who died in 1890. As the many Salvationists "took their stations on a piece of rising ground under the trees facing the grave," the coffin was lifted to a newly erected platform, on which were assembled the "funeral party" and from which the service was conducted.

The two-hour service was, in its inspirational tone, much like any Salvation Army meeting. There was much singing, of songs and choruses so well loved, from "My Jesus, I love Thee, I know Thou art mine" to "Sweeping through the gates of the New

Jerusalem." And the several representative speeches by Commissioners Railton, Cox, Ogrim, Higgins and Howard, Commander Evangeline Booth, and Adjutant Catherine Booth were all, in reality, "testimonies" of thanksgiving.

## LUCY'S SOLO

Commissioner Lucy Booth-Hellberg, the General's youngest daughter, was supposed to sing a solo, but when she rose from her seat and came forward her voice failed her and she wept. In tearful broken sentences she said: "I would like to sing for you . . . Just before he died the General stretched out his hand to take mine . . . He could not see it, but when he grasped it, he said, "Sing to me." "So I sang this song to him . . . I cannot sing it now, dear people . . . You will forgive me? Will you sing it with me?" "So all the people sang," wrote a compassionate reporter, "an old familiar hymn, but it was all a failure, a beautiful failure, because they were crying too."

General Bramwell Booth then gave a short address: "He said that nothing they could say could add anything to the value of what the General did in his life, but they were there to pay their tribute of affection and respect to his memory before the cold ground closed over his body. Today they were burying the father of the Salvation Army and its prophet. He was both a prophet and a seer. No matter what the future of the Army in the world might bring of progress and of victory—and he believed it had a great work before it—there could never again be anybody who would be quite the same to it as its great founder and inspirer. He was their champion.

"He did not say that the late General was never defeated, but he never gave up. His faith in God was great, and he thought he was the happiest man he had ever known. His was a glad spirit, and he carried joy wherever he went. He came out into the arena of affairs risking the rough and tumble of the world, and his wonderful gift of observation, his extraordinary industry and his missionary voyages made him a man who knew and understood the world. He appealed to those who remained behind to follow in their leader's footsteps, to be lovers of the Salvation Army, and to cling to it" [Times].

When Commissioner Eva stepped forward to say a few words, she broke down and sobbed bitterly. "He was everything to me!" she cried. Then some officers led her stumblingly back to her seat, as men and women in the crowd cried out, "Oh, now I believe!" "The dead General," stated a reporter, "had made his last converts."

And, finally, as Colonel Fred Cox stood at the head of the open grave, holding the "Calvary" flag, and, as the vast congregation sang, "Servant of God, well done!" the coffin, with cap and Bible, was lowered into the vault. The service closed with a prayer by Commissioner Oliphant of Switzerland, and then the great assembly dispersed, many of them to make their way to the Clapton Congress Hall where a great evening holiness meeting was soon to commence.

Summing up the day's events, a reporter for *The Daily Chronicle* had this to say:

> *Some of us there, the lookers-on—the reporters of life—had seen the funerals of kings and princes; had watched many strange scenes of history, but never before had any of us seen such a burial as this, or such drama of reality. It was a mingling of triumph and gladness with personal and poignant grief. It was a passionate tribute to the glory of a great man, and a humble assertion of faith before God. It was a proclamation to the world of a work born of the genius of this man whose dust lay coffined there, but also the outpouring of sorrow by a family bereft of its chief. It was the homage of an Army joyous in the thought of victories won by their departed General, but stricken with an intimate and individual emotion at the thought that never again would they see that splendid old figure who had been their inspiration, their prophet, their great captain, their friend (Aug. 30).*

*"I'd stand on my head on top of St. Paul's Cathedral if I thought it would help anybody."*

## CHAPTER SEVEN

# "I Remember William Booth"

Among the public tributes which appeared in the world's newspapers and magazines, were many personal reflections and reminiscences by people who had known William Booth—both non-Salvationists and Salvationists. They took advantage of the moment—or were asked by leading journals—to offer their memories of the remarkable personality and what he meant to ordinary people. Philip Gibbs, who knew Booth quite well and had interviewed him often, contributed his memory of him to his newspaper, *The Daily Chronicle,* which had always been very kind to the Army.

In *The Christian World,* Maurice Whitlow, a Salvation Army officer, told the world what William Booth had meant to him as a follower of his cause. And somewhat later, the Reverend Thomas Rippon, a Methodist Minister, Mrs. Archibald Mackirdy, a social reformer, and the Rev. R.J. Campbell, all of whom had known the General in some capacity or another, shared their memories of the Army's leader.

# "THE LAST REVIEW: AN IMPRESSION"

### Philip Gibbs
#### *The Daily Chronicle* (August 21, 1912)

I have been privileged to have many meetings with "the General," as he was always called by his followers. I have been scolded by him, as a scapegoat of all the journalists with whom he had some bone to pick; I have been forced down upon my knees while he prayed fervently aloud that God might soften the hearts of editors and inspire proprietors with generous instincts; and I have watched him many times putting his spell upon great audiences of rough men and simple women, so that they laughed with him and wept with him.

No one ever left his presence without realizing that here was an old man whose vitality of mind and spirit was abnormal and bordering upon the superhuman; that in those old man's eyes, almost sightless at the last, there burned strange fires of mystical love, of fanatical enthusiasm, of fierce hatred for all that he swept together in his definition of sin.

I have seen him in many moods, and they were as varied almost even in one hour as the scale of human emotion, but in spite of the ordinary flaws of character which little men may discover, quickly enough, in great ones an egotism which demanded flattery and homage, a hard business instinct, an almost cynical sense of humor—the power and ability of the old man rose triumphantly above those weaknesses, and one's imagination was stirred by the personal magnetism, which seemed to flow and flash from him.

## Royal Albert Hall

The last time I saw the old man was on the day before his last operation for cataract in the eyes. It was at the Royal Albert Hall, filled to the uttermost by men and women who serve under his banner, an audience rich in color, wonderfully "stage-managed," as usual with the Salvation Army, and aflame with enthusiasm. Presently into the center of the great living picture there came unto the platform the leader of all these people, and of many hundreds of thousands of other people all over the world whose craving for religious emotion and consolation he has fed with burning words, of whose natural instincts for righteousness he has caught hold out of the depth, dragging them up to decency, to a code of law and order and social service.

He stood there, a tall, frail, old man in black, swaying a little as though the gusts of applause that rose in waves of noise about him actually stirred his body to and fro, as an old tree bends to the wind. His face was almost as white as his great mane, and as the long white beard which flowed upon his black coat, but his eyes burnt with some of their old fire. His soul seemed to light them up, though his first words were a confession that he could not see a face in all that sea of faces, and stood in the blaze of lights as in impenetrable darkness.

Then in a voice that came as a faint, clear whisper through the great hall, where otherwise there was a deep long silence, he told the tale of his life, of his ideals, of his failures, of his achievements, of his hopes. It was a familiar story to everyone there, a story of continual self-sacrifice, of immense endeavor, of a great battle, as he called it, truly enough, with the devils of vice, of selfishness, and of indifference. The long speech in that faint, hoarse whisper, was extraordinary in its egotism.

## Outside Himself

Hundreds of times he spoke the word "I." It began almost every sentence. Yet it was as though he spoke as one outside himself. With no mean little vanity, but with a simple proclamation of the tremendous things attempted and achieved by that General Booth of whom he was telling his people, and of the great drama and character of that man's career. So might Napoleon have spoken when reviewing his past at St. Helena, with such a sublime egotism that it was above self-consciousness.

On that night the old General reviewed his troops for the last time. It was his great farewell. When he ended his speech by a fervent prayer, kneeling down before all the people with only his white hair showing above the platform, men and women wept unrestrainedly. Yet a little while before at quaint little jests jerked into his most solemn retrospection they had guffawed and laughed.

A strange, amazing personality! He would mix buffoonery with spiritual exaltation in a way that shocked people whose religion is kept apart from life, but won the hearts of simple beings, who may laugh and weep in the same half-minute, and confess themselves to God between a breakdown and a cornet solo.

It was his method, partly deliberate, partly in the nature of the man. He had studied the art of arousing popular emotions so that he was a master and could put a wizard spell upon great multitudes. But behind all his little tricks and artistry there was a burning sincerity, a glowing love for humanity in the rough, and unswerving and passionate faith in the Christian ideal.

The secret of the man, after all, is to be found in his faith and work. For that he lived, struggled, conquered, failed, and tried again. After every defeat, and he had many, he went on to the next victory in his great work of social reform and spiritual uplifting. Whatever may have been his faults, he will always remain an heroic figure, and one of the greatest philanthropists of modern times.

## "WHAT HE MEANT TO US"

### Maurice Whitlow
### The Christian World, August 22, 1912: 4

We loved him. There was no slavish fear in our obedience to his orders, no sulky falling in with his commands. He was to us such a living example of all that he preached, so devoted to the cause of the Cross, and because of that, so passionate in his love for humanity that we, his followers, felt compelled to accept his autocracy and fall in with his directions.

We were not deceived, or mistaken, either. Had we been compelled to spend long hours and weeks in conferences and ballotings our work would never have been done. Given the clearsighted General, the undoubted singleness of his life purpose, and the ready obedience of his will to do what he felt to be the divine voice, there is no reason in wavering in response to his call.

## Pragmatism

He set us an example. "Go straight for souls, and go for the worst," he said. And he himself led the way. And, in his eagerness after the souls of men he realized that the line of least resistance was to get at them through their bodies. Like Spurgeon, he knew the difficulty of getting men saved with cold feet and empty stomachs. So he taught us to be practical in our religion, and rather horrified old style evangelicals by insisting on a Gospel of works as well as salvation by faith.

He won our confidence by believing in us. He gave every one of us a platform—or a duty. Throughout the world there is not a single simple Salvationist that has not got some share in the work of the Army. Many of us are not overly bright mentally, most of us are poor in this world's goods, we are for the greater part unlearned and ignorant men and women, yet there is a work for every one of us—not undefined, nebulous sort of work, but a task with duties outlined—and orders and regulations clearly indicated.

Then he taught us the value of woman's work and the soundness of her judgment in matters affecting the everyday work of the individual. That was a wonderful lesson. And he gave practical proof of his belief in womanhood by placing women on an equality with men in the government of the Army. No Salvation Army soldier can ever think lightly of the women's question. Most of us owe more than we can ever estimate in our lives to the women of the Army, who were given their rightful place by General Booth.

But it is impossible for anyone to say, in so brief a space, and with the great sense of our loss still upon us, how much we owe to him, and what he meant to us. He has built our homes and restored our lost ones. He has, by the very autocracy of his rule, banished intoxicating liquors from hundreds of thousands of tables. Erring daughters and wayward sons have been brought home. Criminals have been turned into honest, God-fearing citizens—and we, the soldiers of General Booth's Army, know why and how. These are things that are hidden from the wise and prudent, but have been revealed to us by the teaching and example of our General.

## The Victory

And if, in writing thus, I have said too much of the man, and too little of his God, it is not because I have forgotten the source of his power and the reason of his flaming love. General Booth was all that he was to us because of that great central fact. He brought us, cynical, careless, drinking, thieving, swearing and degraded though many of us were, to that place called Calvary.

To us he made the meaning of Gethsemane clear, and into our hearts he sent the realization of the victory and the Resurrection. That is why we will not half-mast our flags today, but rather we will drape them with white streamers, emblematic of victory. And, when we have followed him to the grave, we will turn again to the work he has shown us how to do, and will try to do it better than ever before.

# "GENERAL BOOTH AS I KNEW HIM"

Rev. Thomas F. Uppon
*The Methodist Times* (August 29, 1912): 4.

The passing away of the General awakens old-time memories. For three years, as a boy, I sat under his ministry, and I have been in intimate touch with him ever since. My earliest recollection of William Booth dates back to the time when he came as superintendent of the Gateshead Methodist New Connexion Circuit (1858, ed.), my father being then identified with that Communion as class-leader and local preacher.

The village chapel, Low Teams, where we worshipped, was often visited by the future General, and his personality greatly impressed me. The remembrance of him is vivid still. His tall, attenuated form, his black hair, his piercing eyes, his commanding speech and flaming earnestness fascinated my youthful imagination and made him my hero. I never missed an opportunity of hearing him, and he never, perhaps, had a more sympathetic admirer.

## Impatient Revolutionary

Booth was a welcome visitor to my parent's home, and we children greatly relished his calls. Humor was one of his characteristics. He was then, as throughout his long career, a man of indomitable will, an autocrat, dogmatic, knowing his own mind and determined upon having it expressed, of marvellous vitality, outspoken, a revolutionary in method, single in aim, resolute. Booth believed in crowds but did not always get them. He was impatient if seats were vacant.

At his commencement of his ministry at our village chapel, the congregations were small, sometimes not numbering more than fifteen people on a week night. One Sunday afternoon he counted his congregation publicly and said, "If there are not more people here the next time I come, I'll not preach!" Those were the days of small things. The texts he preached from then were his favorites up to the very end of his public ministry: such as "How wilt thou do in the swelling of Jordan?" "Turn ye, turn ye, for why will ye die?"

Removing to Gateshead, my people attended Bethesda Chapel, a building seating over a thousand people, and which under Booth's ministry became the scene and center of a great revival. When he entered upon his charge the chapel was almost empty, but within a few months it was filled to overflowing. What was regarded novel in those days, "singing band" marched through the streets to advertise the services, in which I joined, and learned my first lessons in evangelism.

## Shy Catherine

Far back under the gallery in the minister's pew sat Catherine Booth, mother of The Salvation Army, and William Bramwell, its present head, a bright boy of seven summers [the event took place in 1860, when Bramwell was just four years old, ed.] Mrs. Booth was in complete sympathy with her husband's evangelistic work, except in not engaging publicly. Booth was anxious his wife should take a leading part in his services, but her timid, retiring disposition led her to shrink from public work. At length, however, she yielded, which resulted in a way that entirely changed the current of her life, and that of her husband's.

And it happened in this wise. One Sabbath morning Booth preached on "Consecration," and pleaded with his people to give themselves afresh to God. Halfway through the service he went so far as to invite believers to the "penitent form" to seek a fuller baptism. As I have said, Mrs. Booth was timid and retiring. She could scarcely speak with freedom in a society class meeting of half a dozen women. And the last person expected to demonstrate that morning was the shy, retiring lady of the minister's pew. "I wait," said the preacher, "to see if anybody will come out for God."

After a pause Mrs. Booth stepped into the aisle and walked to the communion rail. She knelt in silent prayer, and facing the congregation said: "You know me well. I am your minister's wife, and have had rare opportunities of witnessing for Christ. But I have allowed the enemy to seal my lips. From this moment I resolve to live another life." Then, turning to her husband, she said: "You are appointed to preach here tonight. May I join you in the service that I may further bear my testimony?" "Be it known," said Booth, "and tell it throughout the town, my wife will preach."

## Catherine Lights the Fire

It is difficult to conceive the consternation and excitement that the incident occasioned. I attended the memorable service. The chapel was densely crowded. Booth ascended the pulpit, accompanied by the timid lady, dressed in black, and wearing a white straw bonnet with yellow silk strings. Announcing her text, she preached for an hour, the power of God attending the word so that a revival broke out which spread over the whole county. In the consecration of Catherine Booth that Sabbath morning was the genesis of the Salvation Army.

Speaking of the occasion afterwards, she said: "There was more weeping in the chapel that day than on any previous occasion. Many dated a renewal of righteousness from that very moment, and began a life of devotion and consecration to God. But oh, how little did I realize how much was then involved! I never imagined the life of publicity and trial that it would lead me to, for I was never allowed to have another quiet Sabbath when I was well enough to stand and speak. All I did was to take the first step."

The rest we know. William Booth now saw that his work should not be restricted to any mere circuit boundary. He appealed to the Conference for an appointment as Connexional evangelist, which was refused. His resignation followed. The Booths then went to Cornwall on a revival campaign. A great fire was lighted which blazed throughout the Duchy.

After months of labor in the West, the evangelists traveled to London and took their stand in Whitechapel, where the Christian Mission was founded, which developed into the Salvation Army. The movement grew and wakened world-wide interest. Opposition was fierce. Its soldiers were pelted with refuse, stoned, imprisoned. In spite of it all Booth waged the "holy war," his wife being the brain and silver tongue of the movement.

Never a day free from pain, a malignant disease brought the "Army mother" to her death. It was a far cry from the memorable day at Gateshead when the minister's wife preached her first sermon to the scene in London where from Queen Victoria Street to Abney Park Cemetery hundreds of thousands witnessed the funeral procession. I stood on the pavement outside Headquarters, and saw the coffin, and the grey-haired General, and I heard the sobs of ragged and hungry people who mourned as if the light of their life had gone out.

## Wesleyan Influence

Of the Salvation Army itself I have been a friendly critic and helper. Time will prove whether the organization as at present constituted will work to its advantage. What Wesley was in his day in autocratic leadership, General Booth has been; and possibly in the evolution of things the Salvation Army may be placed on a representative basis. William Booth was an admirer of the Wesleyan system of Church government.

We discussed the matter one night by my dining-room fire when he expressed himself in favor of the "one-man government," given that "the man" could be found, endorsing in that connection what Carlyle said of the true *Papa*, Pope or Father in God, "to whose will our wills are to be subordinated; find me the Konning, King, or able man, and he *has* a divine right over me."

We also discussed the question of union with Methodism, which led to an interesting correspondence with Hugh Price Hughes and the General, of which I was the intermediary. Hughes wrote a favorable article in *The Methodist Times,* and in one of his letters he said:

> *Our people would hail with delight some federal relationship which preserved the General's freedom of action, and at the same time enabled us all to act together. Booth appreciated the kindly sentiments, and whilst favoring union felt "that the day for giving practical*

*expression to it had passed, at least for the present." And there the matter ended.*

*When the "Darkest England" scheme was launched, I was then at Putney, where I organized an effort which realized over £300. When the evening meeting was over, Booth, being my guest, spoke with deep feeling of the criticism to which he was then being subjected by Huxley and others. "We shall come out all right," he said. "My only fear is lest our social work should swamp the spiritual. We must keep before our people more vividly than ever the salvation of souls."*

*Next morning he sat down in my study chair, and wrote this sentence in my album: "In the face of every possible opposition, whether it come from earth or hell, we must go forward to save the bodies and souls of men from misery here and hereafter."*

*It was my privilege to meet the General on several occasions during the last few years. Our last meeting was at the Congress Hall, Clapton. Hearing I was in the audience he sent a messenger to invite me to his side on the platform. The affectionate greeting and blessing of the grand old man are now among my treasured memories.*

## "THE SOLDIER OF SALVATION"

### Mrs. Archibald Mackirdy
### The Christian Globe (August 29, 1912): 23

On a waning afternoon some years ago I went to see General Booth at his home at Hadley Wood to talk with him on the possibility of getting shelters for respectable women and girls. It was by the General's own invitation I went to see him. He had read my book, "The Soul Market," some time before, and had written to thank me for it. At that time the public opinion was against cheap hostels and shelters for women—the argument being that by providing such places homes would be broken up, women be encouraged to defy the discipline and restraint of "home life," and above all that by providing cheap hostels and shelters a great encouragement would be given to prostitution.

The General was in his office when I arrived, and I was immediately taken to him by his secretary. He rose and held out both his hands looking down at me with a tenderly, fatherly smile—the clasp of his hands was firm and warm. "God bless you," he said, several times, and "What a soldier!" He made me sit close beside him, and talked of all the sorrows of the outcast and homeless. "I know it all," he said. The tears dimmed his eyes—and for a few minutes he sat silent, praying. I seemed to feel a spirit of courage and pity encompass me. Never have I met so magnetic a personality.

## Compassion

The curious part of the business is that I went to see the General not quite believing in his utter goodness and kindness. I was prejudiced. I had been at two of his meetings, and was quite untouched. Moreover, there were many who said hard things of him. I knew he must be clever, and capable, and that he *could* help if he cared. The question in my mind was, would he care for anything so unsensational, so humble as helping a few desolate friendless women? I had not been quite with him more than a quarter of an hour when I realized his chivalry, his absolute truth, his divine pity. There was no pleading to do here. He *knew it all*. I felt poured into me a new faith, new life.

Just as some timid recruit facing the enemy's guns for the first time might feel the magic and strength of his general's presence—one who knew, one who had fought, one who had led "forlorn hopes" to make them victories—so I felt in the presence of this Soldier of Salvation—who for thirty years had been leading "Forlorn Hopes" to victory. It is only of late years that the Salvation Army has ceased to suffer persecution—indeed, not even now are these devoted people set free from calumny and misrepresentation—and he—utterly devoted—living an austere and devoted life, was constantly, to the last, accused of amassing wealth and abusing his power.

## God's Knight

When I was with him I learned his spirituality and nobility—
a champion of the down-trodden, a knight of God in his attitude
towards women. He said to me that it tortured him to think of delicate and refined girls driven into temptation, then "herded with
the coarse and dirty scum of the city"; those were his words. He
knew what dire poverty and friendlessness meant to a woman. It
was not that his heart did not yearn over the utterly base and lost.
He was a Soldier of Salvation, and he hungered for the redemp-
tion of these. But he knew all the frightful taint and uncleanness
that sin leaves in its track, and he was wise as well as holy. He
wanted the *unspoiled* to be kept pure, and given a chance.

That wonderful afternoon will live in my mind always. It is a
great thing to be in the presence of holiness and to see the love of
God made manifest in a soul.

Whatever tribute is paid to this great Soldier of Salvation—
this above all, must be remembered of him. When others saw
only difficulties, and imagined dangers, General Booth said: "I
yearn over these women, and would shelter them always—may
God open the way."

He made me have tea with him, and then he prayed. The tears
fell from his eyes, and I simply put down my head on the table
and wept for joy, and because another "Forlorn Hope" was to be
undertaken. There will stand by his grave some of the "first fruits"
of that Home which but for his chivalry, and the assurance that he
would support and keep it, I would never have dared to labor for.

## Homeless Women

No one else at that time believed that such Homes were possible—nor even that they were needed. General Booth *knew the
need,* and he believed that they would be great blessings to many.
He was not *afraid to help the homeless woman* and to champion her
cause. He was afraid of *nothing* but sin, and he was too good a

general to underestimate the power of "the enemy." I loved him then for his great courage, his chivalry, his glowing faith—his passion of pity for all the suffering, beaten creatures.

The greatest of all his work is this, that he has made and left behind such a band of workers that the world has never seen. No man has made out of wastrels soldiers of salvation as he has done. No others but his trained and devoted soldiers have ever gone to dwell among the awful slums of our cities—they went with their lives forfeited to God. That tremendous fervor and hunger for souls, that divine pity—which he inspired in the hearts of men and women of his day, have redeemed thousands to God. These soldiers of his carried the standard into the strongholds of Satan, and fought a way out again. They dismantled the guns of the enemy when they went, and left love for hate, order for disorder, life for death.

That *one* man, poor and obscure, should be given such power of God, has its lessons for us. The great things of life lie not in the hands of the proud and powerful. They lie in the hands of the chosen of God. His death—rather the change of command—for he qualified for vaster service, wakes in us not regret, but magnificent gratitude, that our eyes have seen the miracle of God in that valiant life! Littleness seems to slip away; small personal strivings to die down; there seems nothing better that we can think of doing just now than just to remember the lesson of the General's life—"All things are possible with God," and march on.

## "GENERAL BOOTH: A MEMORY OF MY LAST CHAT WITH HIM"

Rev. J.E. Shephard
The Christian Endeavour Times
(Sept. 12, 1912): 809.

In the homegoing of General Booth there has passed out of the religious activities of the world one of the Church's greatest leaders. He was born to lead, he was called to lead. Some speak of him as an ordinary man taken hold by God and used for His glory. But a careful study of the qualities and characteristics of the man show that he must be classed with the great geniuses. He was great by nature and made greater still by grace. Men have formed various estimates of his worth and work, but time will reveal more than we have ever yet known of the grandeur and stability of his great work . . .

In our last conversation, some twelve months ago, he told of the fights he had had at Castleford in the early days of the Army and the many victories won. It was but a sample of what took place throughout the country and throughout the world. In that last conversation he recalled his early days spent in places common to us both. To recount it is practically to tell the story of his life. There was a tremendous distance between his Nottingham days and mine, but during my brief work I came in contact with many who had known him and worked with him.

## Caughey

We talked of James Caughey, under whose powerful word he had been led to decide for Jesus Christ, and of Wesley Chapel. One of the memories of my childhood, which still survives, is the tall, stern James Caughey standing erect in the pulpit of the church where I was brought up, and stretching out a long bony finger, while he announced his text, "This year shalt thou die." The manner in which he gave out his text struck terror into our young hearts. It was a wonderful time of decision.

In such a time as that, probably when James Caughey had even greater power, for he was an old man when I heard him, William Booth was brought to Jesus Christ, and consecrated himself to His service. Like most of those who are led to decision during great religious awakenings he commenced to evangelize. He was fifteen, and soon became a preacher and soul-winner.

My next recollection which I recalled was a scene in the Hall at Whitechapel Road. In my boyhood I had made the acquaintance of one of his helpers in the Christian Mission, a Mr. Wiggan. This man was an evangelist and he sought to persuade me to join the mission; but my work lay in a different direction. In the hall I remember seeing Mr. and Mrs. Booth sitting on the platform and the late Richard Weaver had charge of the meeting. The General listened to my story of that memorable meeting, his face shining all the while, and at its close he said, "forty years ago." Those were the beginnings, he took up the thread and recounted his trials and triumphs of the succeeding years.

The last interview in my own dining room revealed the true greatness of the general and told the secret of his power. He was so approachable, frank, genial. Full of humor, and repartee. We managed somehow or other to drift into politics, the General rose, and with a merry twinkle of the eye, said, "It is time for me to go to rest now." How wonderful it was to hear him talk with God. As he sat at the table after we returned from the meeting, just like a little child who had received a present from his father, he told God how grateful we were for a wonderful service. It does not matter that we cannot recall the words of his prayer, its manner and spirit will live with us as long as memory lasts.

## A Charming Autocrat

Some speak of him as a great autocrat; no doubt he was, and here was the secret of his success. But who objected to his autocracy? It was so charming, the way in which he gave his orders, the magnetism of his personality seemed to get into his words, his tones, and you never complained of being ordered by him. His autocracy was that of a great general and commander, and of an order which the great democracy still needs. He trusted himself, only as he trusted God. It was his superb faith in God's call to service which gave him his authority. He knew that he was called of God for the work, and would not allow any man to turn him from his course . . .

Like him in our work for the Master may we be at it, always at it, not prevented by discouragements but always looking for victory because the work is God's. It was doubtless this thought which upheld and inspired him when everything seemed against him. The work is God's.

## "WILLIAM BOOTH: AN APPRECIATION"

### Rev. R.J. Campbell
*in The Life of General Booth [1912]*

It is too late in the day to attempt anything like a vindication of the character and methods of the founder of the Salvation Army, the danger to his reputation, if such there is, is rather to be found in the tumultuous and indiscriminate eulogies of which he has been subject since the moment when Royalty gave a belated recognition to his world-wide services in the cause of downtrodden humanity. It is no more necessary to defend General Booth now—except from his friends—than it is necessary to defend Jesus.

### Greatness and Zeal

His name has become one to conjure with, a symbol for moral greatness and self-sacrificing zeal. He had not to wait for death in order to be canonized, for that consummation has been rapidly in progress during the last ten years, and probably he would rather have dispensed with it. As a rule it is a sign that a man's work is done, and that vested evils have no longer much to fear from him. No saint has ever been worth canonizing who either desired or valued it.

But was he a saint? That depends upon our use of the term. He has at least as much title to it as some of those to whom it has been most willingly accorded. If by a saint be meant one who has subdued all earth-born passion, and dwells habitually in holy calm and contemplation, then I suspect that General Booth was not a saint. If, on the other hand, a saint be one whose human energies are devoted to high impersonal ends, then the world has seen few greater . . . Yes, the subject of this sketch was a saint, not because he differed greatly from the common run of man in his spiritual endowments, but because of the use he made of them.

It is impossible for any onlooker to see right into the soul of any servant of God, just as it is impossible to estimate character from achievements; and it may be that in intrinsic moral worth, measured by sheer self-devotion to a divine ideal, there are privates in the Salvation Army nearer to the heart of great things than their General ever was; but a man in whom great forces combine must be worthy of his task, or else it would not be his. And, judging from what we can see of the stupendous soul-liberating effects of the work of the Salvation Army, its organizer and director must have been in extraordinary degree a man of God.

## Born to Lead

I only saw General Booth once. It was on the occasion when he received the freedom of the city of London—a memorable moment in his great career. I was so placed that I could watch every movement of his face while he was listening as well as speaking, and I found myself involuntarily studying the personality rather than attending to what was being said. The first impression one received was that of immense force of character in the man who was the central figure in the great assembly. He was a born leader of men, one not only accustomed to command, to show other people what to do and put them upon doing it by the sheer imperative of his presence—a man of action unquestionably, whose every change of pose suggested inexhaustible physical energy.

To hear him speak was a revelation, too. He had not a single note, his utterance was rapid, but the sentences were faultless; never once did he pause for a word or depart from the main thread of his argument. The speech was longer than is customary on such occasions, but he held the audience enthralled to the finish, many of those present afterwards expressing their astonishment both at the loftiness of sentiment and purity of diction which characterized it throughout. They had expected something quite different—the slipshod utterance of the half educated demagogue, but discovered instead an orator of the first rank.

For a man of the General's age this Guildhall address was a feat worthy of record. This dawned upon me afterwards, for at the moment it was the man himself who interested me. This combination of titanic energy with high moral purpose and pureness of motive was one I never met before in any one man. This man's sincerity had been tested in every possible way through long years of persecution and contempt; he had deliberately chosen a way of reaching the masses which laid him open to the charge of quackery, sensationalism, and irreverence. He had been accused of demoralizing the people he sought to help, vulgarizing religion, seeking cheap notoriety, and what not.

He had not been spared even the suspicion of seeking to enrich himself at the expense of the credulous fools who believed in him and his mission. He had been ostracized from the fellowship of all the orthodox communions, few of which gave him any countenance until he no longer needed it. Yet there he was, having lived it all down and become the mightiest force of his time in bringing the gospel of Jesus into living touch with the needs of the poorest and most degraded elements in the community, not in England alone, but in every quarter of the globe. This triumph had been achieved without leaving in him one trace of bitterness towards those who had wronged and ill-treated him in the days of his humiliation, or one touch of ostentation in his modes of reference to it.

It was an inspiration to look into the face of the grand old man of whom this could be said, and to realize that he was a scarred veteran fresh from a campaign which had lasted over sixty years, and in which he had neither sought nor won a single advantage for himself. Somehow one did not feel that General Booth belonged to the order of prophets and seers. His genius was of the practical kind, informed by a genuine solicitude for the welfare of humanity and fired by faith in God.

## Grace

One wonders what he might have been had the last-named factor been omitted from his experience of life. That he would still have been a leader of men is indubitable, but that he would have been their benefactor is less certain. The impression he formed upon me was that the benevolence in his character was due less to nature than to grace. He would have succeeded in any walk of life by his strength of will and practical insight, but it is quite possible that if his energies had been turned into purely business channels he might have become what the world calls a hard man. That fine head, like Michaelangelo's Moses in its noble outline, could have crowned a great financier; that mobile face, with its revelation of high purpose and brave endeavor, contained suggestions of something not less forceful but less exalted.

It was well for the world that the soul of William Booth was captured by the Spirit of Christ instead of the spirit of mammon. I believe he has himself confessed somewhere that within him he had all the instinct of possession, the tendency to grasp and accumulate material good. He says he inherited it. It may be so; certainly if he had indulged it he would have been a success— perhaps a sinister one. As it was, he died poor, and the world honors in him the sanctified use of the very qualities which would have enabled him to die rich.

*"Be it known, and tell it throughout the town, my wife will preach."*

## CHAPTER EIGHT

# "The Greatest Apostle of the Age?"

When a great man dies, it is very common to consider the nature of his achievements and to speculate on the future without him. It is no surprise, therefore, to find, among the many eulogies, and even in addition to them, many thoughtful assessments of William Booth's career as evangelist and humanitarian, and as many opinions regarding the future of the Army. The three questions most often asked, and usually put very bluntly, were these: "How great was this man?" "What was the secret of his success?" and "What is the future of the Army now that he is gone?"

In answer to the first question, most commentators were simply extravagant in their assessments. "We cannot at this moment recall any man of this generation," wrote the editor of the Philadelphia *North American,* "whose death would have meant so much to so many in so many lands. General Booth belonged to the world in a larger sense than it could have been said of any of his contemporaries."

For his courage in the face of early antagonism and the scorn of both clergy and public spokesmen like Thomas Huxley; for his devotion to a cause that could only be described as "fanatic"; and for having brought the Army from a small tent-sized organization to a world-wide evangelical and social mission, the public now placed him "on a plane with the greatest philanthropists and Christians of all time."

## ONE OF THE GREATS

"He belonged," said the *Congregationalist*, "with such men as Dwight L. Moody and Phillips Brooks, John Wesley and George Fox. Cromwell, Luther, and Bernard, Loyola and Augustine, Peter and Paul." William Booth was, suggested the Chicago *Continent*, one of the "greatest servants of Christ and benefactors of men whom all the centuries have produced." When some chose to make their comparison more specific, or to amplify their reasons for that comparison, their choice inevitably fell on John Wesley.

Some non-partisan writers ranked Booth on equal terms with Wesley, and a few even argued his influence far surpassed that of the great Methodist. The New York *Examiner,* for instance, credited Him with "a giant power hidden away somewhat efficient to achieve things that *dwarf* the work of even men like John Wesley." Most Methodist commentators, however, would not go that far. It was impossible, wrote the editor of *The Methodist Times,* "to refrain from comparing and contrasting the career of General Booth with that of John Wesley," but one had to be cautious of according a greater stature to the former, whose organization was not yet assured of the permanence of Methodism.

That both Booth and Wesley shared the "same unquenchable evangelism and marvelous vitality"; that both were individualists, marking out for himself a distinctive path; that both founded great religious organizations, were matters of certainty. But, Wesley was a scholar, an Oxford don, with a temperamental love of order and restraint, while Booth had little education and "an immense contempt for orderliness and usage in matters ecclesiastical."

And, while Wesley "provided for the continuation of his work by means of a form of government which was representative," Booth had simply "deputed his autocratic" powers to a successor who might not have the ability to continue the work as the Founder had (Aug. 22). Most Wesleyan journals were of a similar opinion: though reluctant to give Booth precedence over Wesley, they nevertheless acknowledged that he had exhibited the "happiest blend of spiritual fervor and social enthusiasm known to the world *since* the days of John Wesley."

## NO COMPARISON

A few commentators believed that comparisons were pointless: that William Booth was unique and possessed qualities which set him apart from other great men. "His career," stated the London *Daily News*, "has that quality of independence and isolation which is the hallmark of great creative minds. It owed nothing to others; it was indifferent to conventions and traditions and schools; it flashed across the sky on an orbit of its own that nothing could deflect. He began his amazing crusade amidst the brickbats and ribaldry of the East End, he ended it amidst the sanction of the whole world; but throughout he remained careless of the verdict of men. He was alone with an idea that burned white heat and consumed all that lay in his path" (Aug. 21).

The allusion to the "brick-bats", and the implicit contrast between the reception accorded the Salvation Army just a decade or two earlier and that registered at Booth's funeral, was itself a matter of much comment. "It will be within the recollection of most who read these lines," wrote *The Daily Graphic*, "that General

Booth was at one time a kind of Guy Fawkes to thousands of the British public; his hallelujah lasses, his sounding brass and tinkling cymbals met with abuse that was something more than vulgar. It was intellectual abuse, pointed by such biting phrases as Huxley's "corybantic Christianity."

It was pointed out that in the 1880s, and early 1890s, Salvationists, mainly on their street marches, had been subjected to a barrage of violent physical assaults, resulting in many of them being severely injured and, often unjustly thrown in jail. They, and their leader, William Booth, had been labeled "dancing dervishes," castigated as "antiChristian fanatics," and generally vilified as being "grotesque," "rowdy" and "irreverent."

Newspapers then were not at all reluctant to classify the Army as a "social nuisance." A case in point was *The Saturday Review* which through the 1880s had waged a bitter war against the Army, calling it a "mixture of blasphemy and buffoonery," adding that anyone who observes the "cult of the ugly, the coarse, the profane, the idiotic, which [the Army] nourishes," could not fail to be disgusted by it. The whole thing was nuisance enough even when confined to its own barracks, but when "it forces its loathsome pagan orgies on the ears and in the way of the public, its shrift cannot be too short or its sentences too long" (July 13, 1889).

## CHANGE OF SENTIMENT

Contrast that with the many tributes which, just two decades later, hailed William Booth as "one of the great religious leaders in Christendom" and we see how far the tide of opinion had turned in the Army's favor. "Thirty years ago," wrote the New York *Nation*, "representatives of every official religious organization in England were rivaling one another in sneering condemnation of the methods of the self-styled General and his Salvation Army, with its trumpets and tambourines, its mock uniforms, its threatenings of hell-fire, and its blasphemous familiarity with the Deity. Now, when the man whose restless energy called this vast organization into being enjoys respite from his labors, there will scarcely be found a religious body to withhold tribute of praise to the memory of a great man who dedicated his life to the service of Christianity" (Aug. 29).

The reason for the seemingly sudden change of opinion was not merely that most people were being respectful of the dead, but that, as *The Nation* pointed out, the results of Booth's methods—vulgar though they might have been to some—proved them to be successful. "Such methods may have been vulgar, and, even after their triumphant vindication, the more sensitive may still deplore them, but there is no doubt that they did the work and reached the people whom they were intended to attract—the waifs of the street, the frequenters of the saloon and the dance hall, the criminal and the fallen—with a success that could have been attained by no other means. Just as John Wesley aroused the official church from its apathetic indifference to the religious needs of his generation, so did General Booth show religious bodies how it was possible to penetrate into the by-ways and dark alleys of modern life."

"To those who remember the early days of the Salvation Army," stated *The Methodist Times,* "with the contempt and opposition it aroused, the change of sentiment must appear little short of a miraculous transformation. It says much for the good feeling and good sense of the public, which, though it may be prejudiced and suspicious to begin with, is ready to accord a generous tribute of praise when once it has been convinced of the high aims and the beneficent work of those whom it has misjudged.

"It is a striking witness to the widespread demand for a faith that counts, and for a religion that means business. Those who take a despondent view of the spiritual outlook of the present day may well be encouraged by the proof that has begun throughout the last week that, after all, nothing interests men so much as an example of the Christian religion greatly lived" (Aug. 29).

## PUBLIC RECOGNITION

A true indication that this adulation was not being expressed simply out of respect for the dead was the fact—one pointed out by a number of commentators—that William Booth had, in recent years, been deservedly recognized as a great public benefactor. In 1902 the Army had been invited to send a representative to Edward VII's coronation; in 1904 he had been accorded a private audience with the King; in 1905 he received the Freedom of the City of London; and in 1907 he was made an Honorary Doctor of Civil Law by Oxford University. He was by then being hailed as "one of the great religious leaders in Christendom."

The real difficulty, in all this, was to answer the second question, "What was the secret of William Booth's success?"

A few commentators preferred to believe that Booth possessed one personal attribute above others, which marked him as a man bound to succeed. Some seemed to favor the suggestion that it was his "genius for organization" which established The Salvation Army as a foremost religious denomination. As the *Congregationalist* put it, "the greatest captain of industry, the most expert professor of the modern gospel of business efficiency might profitably have sat at the feet of this plain and consecrated Christian man."

Harold Begbie, who professed a close acquaintance with the General, adamantly rejected that theory:

> There is one common illusion concerning General Booth. The vulgar sneers are forgotten, the scandalous slander that he was a self-seeking charlatan is now ashamed to utter itself except in vile quarters; but men still say—so anxious are they to escape from the miracle, so determined to account for every great thing by little reasons—that his success as revivalist lay only in his powers as an organizer. Now nothing is further from the truth. General Booth was not a great organizer, not even a great showman. He would have

*ruined any business entrusted if his life had been spent on that side of the operations.*

*Far from the hard, shrewd, calculating, and statesmanlike genius of the Army's machinery, General Booth has always been its heart and soul, its dreamer and its inspiration. The brains of the Army are to be looked for elsewhere. Bramwell Booth is the man of affairs. Bramwell Booth is the master mind directing all those worldwide activities. And but for Bramwell Booth the Salvation Army as it now exists, a vast catholic organization, would be unknown to mankind.*

*General Booth's secret, so far as one may speak about it at all, lay in his perfectly beautiful and most passionate sympathy with suffering and pain. I have met only one other man in my life who so powerfully realized the sorrows of other people. Because General Booth realized those sorrows so very truly and so very actually, he was able to communicate his burning desire for radical reformation to other people. The contagiousness of his enthusiasm was the obvious cause of his extraordinary success, but the hidden cause of this enthusiasm was the living, breathing reality of his sympathy with sorrow (Daily Chronicle, Aug. 22).*

Though stating the matter in different terms, many commentators seemed to agree with Begbie, arguing that it was Booth's "magnetic personality," his imaginative impulse and his single-minded devotion to his dream which marked him as a "man above other men." "Many men have thought," remarked the editor of *The Methodist Times*, "they discovered his secret in a genius for organization. It is quite likely that they were mistaken." And even if that were so, the writer argued, the explanation would be insufficient. "The mere organizer is not a creator. He must have something given to him to organize. That something must consist in truth and life called into new activity by an outstanding personality.

"And General Booth was that. Conditions of all kinds were against him. His drawbacks and deficiencies were obvious. Yet he had the one supreme gift, and before it all else became but as chaff before the wind. General Booth believed, above all things, in his God, in himself, and in his commission. He believed, so unquestionably and so fearlessly that he knew nothing of half measures, was heedless of ridicule, and turned all kinds of opposition into fresh instruments of his own over-mastering and victorious purpose" (Aug. 29).

## PASSION FOR PEOPLE

It was his passion, then, his single-mindedness, which set him apart from the ordinary preacher. Here is how the London *Daily News* put it: "But though the first impression was that of a business instinct, the underlying passion that consumed him soon overwhelmed this impression. It was the passion for humanity—for the poor and the forlorn, the hopeless and the outcast. It was a passion that took no account of race, creed or color. The world was his parish and he embraced all humanity in his scheme of salvation.

"It was a passion, too, that took no account of intellectualism or theological refinement. What had those things done, what were they doing for the submerged and lost? If the methods of the churches were too respectable and too delicate to reach them then they were condemned. He would go down into the underworld with drum and trumpet, with flags flying, and with shouts of 'Hallelujah!' The polite might be shocked and the comfortable outraged; but what had he to do with the polite and comfortable?" (Aug. 21).

According to this view, the Salvation Army was an expression of and gave expression to Booth's personality. "He had his message," stated the editor of the *Methodist Times,* "and he gave it. Its truth shone out upon him with self-evidencing splendor. He felt no need of either arguments to justify it, or of reason to find its coherence with the nature and history of the universe . . .Thus a harmonious institution and a consistent plan fulfilled and served the great personality that created them both. The work is the self-expression of the man, and proclaims his power to command conditions and control circumstances" (Aug. 29).

More wisely, and perhaps closer to the truth, most commentators suggested that Booth's success resulted not from a single character trait but from a combination of qualities—qualities not often combined in a single person. The editor of the New York *Outlook* was certainly of that opinion:

> It is true that the Salvation Army, which he founded, was not democratic, but military, in its organization and method; but its founder, although an autocrat, was devoted with great singleness of purpose to the welfare of his fellow-men, and cared for theological doctrine and ecclesiastical institutions only as they promoted that welfare. He was a great organizer, and lived to see the organization, which he created, spread throughout the Christian world. He was a great preacher, possessing the power to inspire great masses of men with his own enthusiasm . . .
>
> Not less remarkable than General Booth's ability to inspire and harness the enthusiasm of his followers was his ability to direct it into new channels. The Salvation Army was originally a purely evangelistic organization, having for its aim the conversion of individuals to Christ, and differing from other religious organizations in the more popular, not to say more crude and sensational, methods which it employed. But in 1890, with the publication by General Booth of "In Darkest England and the Way Out" General Booth transformed the Salvation Army from a purely evangelistic into a social and philanthropic organization, still, however, retaining its evangelistic methods and spirit.

## Moral Power

> It is true that this transformation was in accordance with the spirit of the times; but it is also true that the success which it has accomplished throughout so large an organization and over so wide an extent of territory affords a striking demonstration of the moral power of the man . . . We do not recommend the Christian churches

*and the Christian ministry to adopt blindly either the methods or the
doctrines which have characterized the Salvation Army, but they
might well study with advantage to themselves this threefold spirit of
enthusiasm, cooperation, and devotion which has made the Salvation Army so great a power for the betterment of human character
and human conditions (Aug. 29).*

## ZEAL AND FAITH

The London *Daily Express,* though more melodramatic than
that, was also of the same opinion.

*"I'd stand on my head on the top of the dome of St. Paul's Cathedral
if I thought I could help anybody by doing so." That declaration typified General Booth and his methods. To do good, no matter how, no
matter what prejudices he offended—this was his own great aim in
life. He will go down in history as the one supremely great religious
leader of the nineteenth century. He not only possessed the missionary fervor of a Peter the hermit or a Wesley; he also had the
organizing power of a Kitchener, and the business acumen of a
Whiteley. Medieval zeal and supreme unquestioning faith were his,
but so was the acuteness of the modern hustling Anglo-Saxon.*

*The success of his career and the success of his wonderful orga-
nization arose from the fact that, starting out to preach the gospel to
the poor, the uneducated, and the unthinking, he unhesitatingly
adopted the one method—call it the showman's methods if you
will—which was sure to attract their notice. He had, too, that
strange, magnetic attractiveness inseparable from the born leader of
men, allied with an entire absence of self-consciousness, and an almost childlike simplicity, which made willing followers of the most
unlikely subject (Aug. 21).*

And, in a similar vein, the editor of the Toronto *Globe and
Mail* argued that William Booth possessed a number of outstanding attributes that combined to ensure his success:

*A towering personality, a human dynamo, a preacher of compelling conviction, an orator, and, most of all, a man in profound sympathy with the joys and sorrows, victories and defeats of his fellow men, General William Booth, founder and Commander-in-Chief of the most extensive movement in modern times, was all these. No man in the past fifty years touched the imagination of so wide a world. (Aug. 21).*

Notwithstanding the variety of opinions, and even acknowledging that his true "genius" was most evident in his ability to create and sustain a "dual mission," it was universally accepted (even by those who cared little for his religion, but admired his social conscience) that William Booth's religious passion—his desire to see the world (not just the "submerged" but everybody) brought to a knowledge of the "saving power of Jesus Christ" was what gave his life direction.

## A HELPING HAND

Thus, while most commentators, especially those in the United States, were more aware of, and perhaps more in sympathy with, the Army's social work, it was always well understood that William Booth's single motive, and the underpinning of his mission, was to "save people from their sins." His was, as one writer put it, a helping-hand Christianity. Though they might not all have believed his message, they certainly knew what it was, and that it was the foundation of his every action. Their editorials made this quite clear:

*There have been many consecrated and holy men who have given themselves up to the task of seeking and saving the lost—"the submerged masses," as it has been the fashion to call them—but not in years and centuries has a man arisen with the courage, the devotion and the supreme and contemptuous disregard of the world's opinions and prejudices which characterized William Booth (Brooklyn Times).*

*General Booth devised a way of getting religion into the slums, and no one any longer denies that the Salvation Army has rescued thousands and thousands of men and women from lives of vice and destitution and made decent and useful members of society of them. It is a great record for a man to leave behind him (Philadelphia Record).*

*William Booth was a pioneer, and as such will leave the impress of his work upon all nations for years to come. Many organizations and societies had talked about reaching the lowly and degraded and the sinful—the "submerged tenth"—but William Booth was the man who went to them and talked with them, and prayed with them, and ministered to them, and brought them to a realizing sense of their need of God (Colorado Springs, Evening Telegraph).*

*In an age inclined to "put trust in chariots and horses," in machinery, he emphasized the paramount need of a change of heart as the foundation of social reform. He put first things first. The Army has never lowered its banner of "Salvation" (The Church Family Newspaper, Aug. 27).*

## CHARISMA

The chief conviction expressed in all the post-mortem assessments was chiefly this: that the Salvation Army had been brought into existence by the force of William Booth's imagination, personality and faith. It was sustained by his genuine love for the poor, and his unquenchable hope that each of even the basest sort could be made to see the value of giving one's life over to God.

Having persuaded themselves, and the world, that William Booth's personality—his personal and public charisma—was unlikely to be seen again; that his "genius for organization" was equal to that of any modem industrialist; that his preaching style was uniquely powerful; and that his religious passion was unparalleled in the last several decades; the final question was: "Could the Salvation Army survive without the power of that personality?"

There were, of course, and quite understandably so, some reservations and even some negative predictions. *The Church Times*, a High Anglican journal, was among those who were not confident that the Army could continue as vibrantly as it had.

*It is original: in conception and in execution, his work. It remains to be seen whether he has created a thing that can stand without him . . . Time will show; but even now a tentative answer is possible. General Booth set out with no object but to save souls, and above all the souls that seemed most hopelessly lost. He probably believed implicitly the enormous statistics of conversion that were published by credulous and enthusiastic underlings. He probably had an invincible confidence in the steadfastness of converts, which was proof against all evidence of failure. He never went back himself: why should others? But a subtle change has come over his work.*

*We reckon least useful among his activities those which draw most public support. The book called "Darkest England and the Way Out," which he owed in secret to the journalistic genius of the late Mr. Stead, was one of the worst kind ever written; his plans for social betterment were crude and showily inefficient; the public gave him much money to spend on them, but happily not a tithe of what he asked; his shelters and colonies are the despair of rational reformers, and his schemes for emigration have degenerated into a trading agency.*

## Respectable Religion

*Meanwhile the original work of the Army has come to a standstill. There is a large and wealthy organization that now does little but advertise its own existence. Recruits are few, and are drawn for the most part from the vaguely religious. One thing the Salvation Army continues to do, and it does this even better as its procedure has become less grotesque. It keeps the profession of religion visibly before the eyes of thousands who hardly know it in any other form, and on the whole it makes religion a thing respected (Aug. 23).*

Presenting much the same argument, the influential London *Times* also declared that the Army was already showing signs of stagnation and that, with the death of its leader, its slowdown would considerably increase.

> *Everywhere we hear that the Army is not bringing in recruits as fast as of old. Its novelty has worn off; its uniforms are no longer impressive; its street services, though they provoke no opposition, do not seem to attract the wastrel and the "rough" as they did at first. We can readily believe that the work goes on more or less as before; but the gatherings, we suspect, are mostly composed of those who have long frequented them and of a certain number of new members drawn rather from existing sects than from persons till now untouched by religion (Aug. 21).*

There was, among that group, no assertion that the Army would cease to exist, or that its work among the poor and outcast, would discontinue; merely that it would lose its vitality. The *Lutheran* put the matter this way:

> *As a movement independent of the Church, the Salvation Army, stripped of its connection with the Church's historical roots and life, will sooner or later lose the evangelical fire that consumed its founder and become a charity organization chiefly.*

It was generally acknowledged, however, even by the most negative prognosticator, that whatever loss of vitality might occur would be the result of a natural diminution rather than of the loss of its spiritual leader. The obvious decrease of interest in religion, the new materialism of the times, would account for some of that loss, while the assumption of middle-class values on the part of Salvationists themselves, a second-and third generation upward mobility, with its attendant inward-looking attitude, would probably accelerate the decline.

## PASSING THE TORCH

For it was almost universally agreed that the new General, Bramwell Booth, would make a very capable leader. "From the day Mr. Bramwell Booth went down to Whitechapel in 1874," stated *The Christian Globe*, "he has not been away, officially, from the side of the General. He has acted as his amanuensis, printer, editor, financier, chief organizer, principal of Salvation theology, and for the last three decades as Chief of the Staff, or second in command. When the late General went on his world tours he left the whole Army in his son's hands, giving him the necessary power of attorney.

"Not once did he disappoint the General. As teacher he has done more than any other officer to educate the Army. He is responsible for most of the books of regulations. He remolded the training home; it is now a college. He instituted an International Staff College, where all the year round promising men and women from different parts of the world spend a few months in London receiving instruction in the principles and practices of salvation and social warfare" [Aug. 29, 1912].

Though all those attributes may not have been entirely deserved—for many others including his mother Catherine and his mentor, Railton, had played a large role as well—it was certain that no one had a greater knowledge of the internal workings of the Army or a more total grasp of its operations than Bramwell. *The Christian Globe* summed up the universal feeling on the matter this way:

> *Not more than once in a century is it given to a nation to possess a man of the apostolic fervor and genius of the later Leader and Founder of the Salvation Army. He was known throughout the world, and respected, even loved, wherever known . . . His sincerity, his burning zeal and his undoubted self-sacrifice, appealed to all . . . He possessed a spark divine. We may call it genius, or passion,*

*or originality, or what we will. It is hard to define, but not hard to recognize. He was amongst us as a prophet; he led, he saw, he inspired.*

*What especially of him on whose shoulders rests the great responsibility of the Generalship? It is to him we turn now; and we turn to him with confidence. He has the burden of a great name. He may not possess the precise qualities which distinguished his father; but he is no tyro. General Booth, as he is now known, is a man of first-rate qualities. We can no more think of the work of the Salvation Army failing because its founder is taken than we can think of Methodism as dying because John Wesley is gone. God lives. He buries His workmen, but He carries on His work. We hail the new General . . . The God who has raised up the Army can sustain it. This was the faith of its founder; and it is the faith of his successor"* [Sept. 5, 1912].

## DEVOTION AND PASSION

In other words, it was generally conceded that the Salvation Army would survive mainly because the devotion and passion which William Booth had instilled in his troops was so deeply set that it was unlikely to disappear now that he was no longer around to physically inspire them. The dead General's fire, one commentator stated, would continue to burn in the hearts of his soldiers.

It was also argued that since so much of what William Booth had done was so distinctive and original there was little likelihood his followers would want to abandon it for anything less. His was, for example, a life of self-sacrifice and it was on this that Salvationism depended.

*He reckoned on that self-sacrifice [in his followers] and organized it for service. While the churches were too often making the Christian profession easy he ventured to make it hard and exacting. And his faith was justified, as such faith will always be. A multitude of plain men and "Hallelujah Lasses" sprang up all over the world who were ready, at all costs, to bear witness to such a Gospel and to follow such a leader.*

*General Booth brought a fresh revelation that there is an unlimited store of chivalry available, in the unlikeliest quarters, for those who will call it forth in the service of God and man. So far from an easy religion being sought, the truth is that only a heroic and costly religion is really prized, or can avail anything in the world (Methodist Times, Aug. 29).*

## WOMEN

On a very practical level, it was suggested that such distinctive features as brass bands, a military style, and, above all, the prominent participation of women were, in and of themselves, enough to ensure survival. And it was the last of these which was seen to have been (through the enormous influence of his wife) William Booth's most brilliant innovation. Women, stated one commentator, were more attuned by nature to the demands of self-sacrifice and so, "with practical sagacity," Booth took full advantage of the possibilities of female service and "gave thereby a new object lesson of the services that consecrated womanhood can render to mankind."

It was, therefore, almost unanimously agreed that though the Salvation Army would, in the natural way of things, lose some of its vitality, it would survive its leader's death. And though its new General might lack the fiery zeal, the platform "charisma" and the "simple touch" of his father, he was entirely capable of ensuring its continuance as both a spiritual and social force throughout the world.

There were, thought most observers, two main issues facing Bramwell Booth. First and foremost, was how he would deal with autocracy. That it had been a system well-suited to William Booth's method of "control by enthusiasm" was granted; that his son, seemingly less flexible in his assumption of power, would be able to maintain his officers' support under such a system was a question no one could answer. All most would concede was that some changes, especially allowing territories (such as America) more autonomy, seemed to be essential if harmony were to be maintained.

Most commentators also agreed that Bramwell Booth seemed to be more interested in pushing the social work than was his father. Already, it was noted, the Army had changed considerably—was more dedicated to social reclamation than to evangelization—a change which was thought to have been brought about largely through the influence of Bramwell Booth and which was likely to be emphasized under his leadership. It was suggested by many that if this trend towards "humanitarianism" continued, the movement would, sooner or later, lose its evangelical zeal and become chiefly a social-welfare agency.

## A TURNING POINT

Just how prescient those writers were—how well they read the nature of William Booth's influence and the abilities of his son—the histories have shown. It is not our intention here to dwell on whether they were right or wrong, but simply to describe the moment—to demonstrate, through the commentary, just how far along the road to fame William Booth had come and why so many influential people thought that the fame was entirely deserved. And to show that the Salvation Army had, by the time of Booth's death and largely through his selfless devotion, reached the apogee of its orbit. That the future was uncertain was due less to the vacancy which William Booth's death created and more to the fact that the Salvation Army, at that moment, had reached a turning point: it was, to be sure, now a highly respected and, perhaps less reassuring, a respectable religious agency. Its new General would have to face that fact.

At the moment of William Booth's death, however, such considerations were only of secondary interest to most observers. For them, as for thousands of Salvationists, the moment was mainly one of celebration, not denigration—celebration of a great man and his achievements. For "whatever the future may reveal, we can at all events now give grateful thanks to God for the life and work of this noble prophet and preacher who brought light to the dark places of our land, and who spread the glad tidings of salvation among many alien races" (*Methodist Times,* Aug. 22). His death was indeed "swallowed up in victory."

## APPENDIX

# The General's Will

The following is a brief summary of General Booth's testamentary dispositions as officially issued in the London *Times:*

(1) By his will, which (except as to the appointment of his executor and the confirmation of the appointment of his successor) deals only with the properties held by him as General of The Salvation Army or on any like public trusts, he formally vests all such properties, both real and personal, including copyrights, in his successor as the General for the time being of the Army, to be held by him upon the trusts affecting the same.

(2) By three codicils he deals (a) with his small private property, the net value of which amounts to £487 19s [then about $2440]. This he gives to the Salvation Army, with the exception of certain private papers and memoranda which he leaves to his eldest son, the present General; and a few articles, chosen by himself, which he gives as mementoes to his children and children-in-law.

(3) By the codicils the General also (b) deals with property of the present estimated value of £5,295 [then about $26,475],

subject to duties and some expenses, representing moneys which—as is well known—were many years ago settled by the late Henry Reed on the late General for his private use. It was this provision which enabled the late General throughout his life to draw no stipend or remuneration of any kind from the funds of the Salvation Army. The late General divides this settled property amongst his children, Mr. Bramwell Booth—his successor— Catherine, Marian, Herbert, Eva, and Lucy, in exercise of the power given to him by the settlement. He leaves £400 on trust for his daughter, Marian Billups Booth, for life, with remainder to Bramwell Booth; £300 each is left to his daughter, Catherine Booth-Clibborn, and his son, Herbert, and the balance of the fund is left equally between his children, Bramwell, Eva and Lucy.

Legacies to:

Bramwell: the casket in which I received the freedom of the City of London;

Eva, my ring;

Lucy, my square repeater watch;

Comm. Booth-Tucker, the clock in my study;

Catherine: the portrait of myself, and to her husband my green walking-stick;

Ballington: one of the ink-stands from my study table.

(4) By the will the general appoints his successor as his executor.

# Crest Books

### Salvation Army National Publications

*Crest Books, a division of The Salvation Army's National Publications department, was established in 1997 so contemporary Salvationist voices could be captured and bound in enduring form for future generations, to serve as witnesses to the continuing force and mission of the Army.*

Shaw Clifton, *Never the Same Again: Encouragement for New and Not–So–New Christians,* 1997

Compilation, *Christmas Through the Years: A War Cry Treasury,* 1997

William Francis, *Celebrate the Feasts of the Lord: The Christian Heritage of the Sacred Jewish Festivals,* 1998

Marlene Chase, *Pictures from the Word,* 1998

Lyell M. Rader, *Romance & Dynamite: Essays on Science & the Nature of Faith,* 1998

Shaw Clifton, *Who Are These Salvationists? An Analysis for the 21st Century,* 1999

Compilation, *Easter Through the Years: A War Cry Treasury,* 1999

Terry Camsey, *Slightly Off Center! Growth Principles to Thaw Frozen Paradigms,* 2000

Philip Needham, *He Who Laughed First: Delighting in a Holy God,* (in collaboration with Beacon Hill Press, Kansas City), 2000

Henry Gariepy, ed., *A Salvationist Treasury: 365 Devotional Meditations from the Classics to the Contemporary,* 2000

Marlene Chase, *Our God Comes: And Will Not Be Silent,* 2001

A. Kenneth Wilson, *Fractured Parables: And Other Tales to Lighten the Heart and Quicken the Spirit,* 2001

Carroll Ferguson Hunt, *If Two Shall Agree* (in collaboration with Beacon Hill Press, Kansas City), 2001

John C. Izzard, *Pen of Flame: The Life and Poetry of Catherine Baird*, 2002

Henry Gariepy, *Andy Miller: A Legend and a Legacy*, 2002

Compilation, *A Word in Season: A Collection of Short Stories*, 2002

R. David Rightmire, S*anctified Sanity: The Life and Teaching of Samuel Logan Brengle*, 2003

Chick Yuill, *Leadership on the Axis of Change*, 2003

Compilation, *Living Portraits Speaking Still: A Collection of Bible Studies*, 2004

A. Kenneth Wilson, *The First Dysfunctional Family: A Modern Guide to the Book of Genesis*, 2004

Allen Satterlee, *Turning Points: How The Salvation Army Found a Different Path*, 2004

David Laeger, Shadow and Substance: *The Tabernacle of the Human Heart*, 2005

Check Yee, *Good Morning China*, 2005

Marlene Chase, *Beside Still Waters: Great Prayers of the Bible for Today*, 2005

Roger J. Green, *The Life & Ministry of William Booth* (in collaboration with Abingdon Press, Nashville), 2006

Norman H. Murdoch, *Soldiers of the Cross: Susie Swift and David Lamb*, 2006

Henry Gariepy, *Israel L. Gaither: Man with a Mission*, 2006

R.G. Moyles, ed., *I Knew William Booth*, 2007

John Larsson, *Saying Yes to Life*, 2007

Frank Duracher, *Smoky Mountain High*, 2007

R.G. Moyles, *Come Join Our Army*, 2008

Ken Elliott, *The Girl Who Invaded America: The Odyssey Of Eliza Shirley*, 2008

Ed Forster, *101 Everyday Sayings From the Bible*, 2008

Harry Williams, *An Army Needs An Ambulance Corps: A History of The Salvation Army's Medical Services*, 2009

Judith L. Brown and Christine Poff, eds., *No Longer Missing: Compelling True Stories from The Salvation Army's Missing Persons Ministry*, 2009.

*Quotes of the Past & Present*, A Compilation from the *War Cry*, 2009

Henry Gariepy and Stephen Court, *Hallmarks of The Salvation Army*, 2010

John Cheydleur and Ed Forster, eds., *Every Sober Day Is a Miracle*, 2010

R.G. Moyles, *William Booth in America: Six Visits 1886 - 1907*, 2010

Shaw Clifton, *Selected Writings, Vol. 1: 1974-1999 and Vol. 2: 2000-2010*, 2011

*How I Met The Salvation Army*, A Compilation from the *War Cry*, 2011

A. Kenneth Wilson, *It Seemed Like a Good Idea at the Time: Some of the Best and Worst Decisions in the Bible*, 2011